NIGERIA : OUTLINE OF A COLONY

Other Books on the Colonial Empire

First published October 1946
Reprinted 1948

At the Moslem Law School, Kano

NIGERIA

OUTLINE OF A COLONY

C. R. NIVEN

THOMAS NELSON AND SONS LTD
LONDON EDINBURGH PARIS MELBOURNE
TORONTO AND NEW YORK

PREFACE

THIS is the rough outline of twenty years' experience in Nigeria. It does not furnish a complete picture (for who could of so vast a country ?), but it conveys some impression of what the British effort in Nigeria has been, not as summarized in official documents, but as remembered and told by one who has shared in it. Here may be read the troubles and trials, the successes and failures, the laughs and the tears of a young colony : it is a record of men who did not just sit in the shade and drink long cool drinks, but got down to work and laid solid foundations for future development. The record shows too what yet remains to be done.

When reading this book the reader is asked always to keep in mind that though Nigeria is in many respects the greatest of the Crown Colonies, it is also the youngest of them, and, as is often the case with young people, it has throughout been very short of money.

C. R. NIVEN

Lagos 1945

CONTENTS

LIST OF ILLUSTRATIONS

*All the above photos are Crown Copyright Reserved,
with the exception of " Early days in Nigeria," which is
the author's copyright*

Chapter One

SURVEY OF A COLONY

THE greatest of the Crown Colonies, Nigeria, lies on the Bight of Benin, in the hollow beneath the bulge of West Africa. In area, population, and political interest, in diversity of language, scene, and climate, in the dawning advancement of its peoples, and in its all-round future possibilities, the Colony stands almost alone. To seek a fair comparison one must turn, with great deference, to parts of India. Only in wealth does it lag behind some of the others.

To reach Nigeria from the United Kingdom the usual course was to catch the mail boat (Elder, Dempster & Co., Ltd.) from Liverpool. This boat, after steaming south for ten days, passing Madeira and the Canary Islands, called at Freetown on the African bulge, and then, hugging the coast, at Takoradi and Accra on the Gold Coast, to reach Lagos in Nigeria about the sixteenth day. (The Gold Coast and the French Ivory Coast are the survivors of the four ill-omened " Coasts "—the Grain, Ivory, Gold, and Slave coasts—which run in that order under the bulge. Between the Gold Coast and Nigeria lie the old German, now mandated, Colony of Togoland and the French Colony of Dahomey.) From Lagos the boat went on to Port Harcourt in Eastern Nigeria, and Victoria, a picturesque town at the foot of the Cameroon Mountain. Other shipping lines, too, touch at Nigeria, besides the mail line ; the French, Dutch, and Germans used to run good services along the coast, and people often travelled by them for the sake of variety and the good cooking provided.

I

There are several air lines connecting West Africa with Europe and with other parts of Africa—British, French, and Belgian—but before the war their planes were small and accommodation was limited and expensive. Shortly after the war a call at Kano was started by the Belgian, Dutch, and French air lines on their trans-African runs. The BOAC, which began with the coast route, now has its main line running direct from London to Kano, taking sixteen hours.

Such an advance will exert a great influence on the life of the coast, for even remote places will be brought into close touch with the larger centres. People who might formerly have been dissuaded from going to Nigeria by the prospect of isolation will no longer have reason to worry, since there will be much closer contact with Britain and a better possibility of getting home quickly to deal with family emergencies. Already air transport has made some difference; the Nigerian Government seems no longer thousands of miles from Downing Street when officials from the Colonial Office can get out in a short time, and, after discussing affairs with the people on the spot, get back speedily to their desks and *vice versa*.

In the same way high officials will be able to get round the country and see things for themselves, and the bogy of report-writing will diminish, to everyone's advantage. Here is one example of how time can be saved. People often want to go from Lagos to Port Harcourt on business that possibly will not take up more than a couple of hours. The journey can be made by sea in thirty hours, but sailings are infrequent and there is no possibility of a quick return. It can also be made by train, but the distance is over a thousand miles, the journey out and back taking six days. By air one can reach Port Harcourt in an hour and a half and return the same day.

The four Coast Colonies are served by West African

Airways Corporation, financed and controlled by the four Governments. Nigeria has its own air services for local purposes, and an ambitious internal service is being planned.

Before the coming of air transport, people depended entirely on road, river, and railway. The vast majority still rely on these, since their travelling is either over short distances, or not specially urgent, or not served by the air routes. A later section of this book will deal with travel by the ordinary surface means, for it has its own interest.

Size and Population

The area of Nigeria is 373,000 sq. miles, and the population is over 22,000,000. That conveys little impression of their magnitude. It is not until you have tried getting about in Nigeria that you realize just what a vast land it is. It is bigger than Belgium, France, Switzerland, and Italy taken together, with Corsica to boot. Even that may not convey a great deal, since few people realize how vast France is. Put it another way : England and Wales cover 58,000 sq. miles. The area of Nigeria is six-and-a-half times as great. We think of the Indian provinces as huge, but if it were one of them, Nigeria would be the fifth province by virtue of population and the first by virtue of size (being two-and-a-half times the area of Madras, the largest).

The population of Nigeria is small in relation to the area, the average number of people to the square mile being only 59. But this conveys a misleading impression of uniformity, when in fact there are large tracts of the country with over 300 to the square mile and others with under 10. The population was considerably reduced by the slave trade, and it is safe to say that without it there would have been at least 8 million more people in Nigeria to-day. Yet as it is there are more people in Nigeria than in Canada,

Australia, and New Zealand taken together. Since those are young countries and Nigeria is an old one that is not surprising: but what is surprising is that of the total population of 47 millions in the whole of West Africa, from Dakar to Duala and the French Cameroons, no fewer than 22 millions are in Nigeria.

Even then this figure is probably on the low side, since it is based solely on the annual count made for taxation purposes. When people, especially primitive people, are counted for taxation there is a forgivable display of coyness, and a marked tendency to slip away into the bush on the approach of the recording staff! Even that is better than the former welcome with flights of arrows and cascades of beehives down steep mountain paths! And yet the tax is not particularly heavy. From a European point of view seven or eight shillings a male head per annum would not be considered serious, but in Nigeria little money is in circulation; the vast majority of the people do not buy their food but grow it for themselves, using money only for clothes, farm implements, luxuries, and tax.

Nigeria is overwhelmingly an African country, with fewer than 5,000 Europeans of all nations and classes, and very few of them really " living " there. It is a country in which one works and from which one goes home to Britain for leave and finally to retire. Some have homes in both countries, but most have their possessions in Nigeria and their families in Britain. Yet having possessions in Nigeria is apt to prove a burden, since one is likely to be moved frequently from place to place, and then all one's possessions have to be packed up and taken too. This difficulty is officially recognized, and officers are allowed two tons of free transport for their belongings when they move on transfer. Of the five thousand Europeans in Nigeria over two thousand are government servants in all departments and on the railway; missionaries, traders, and miners make up most of the rest. There are no idle folk. Most people work for large-scale employers, though there is a handful of people in individual enterprise. Only on the Plateau do people stay for lengthy periods: some have stayed for years, and indeed a number of miners have built themselves houses and retired there from work. Certain Roman Catholic missionaries, whose lives are of selfless devotion, seldom if ever go home to Britain.

Climate

The frank truth is that the climate is very trying. It is not as grim as some have made out, yet it is not one in which white people can stay indefinitely without becoming enervated. Despite this, with proper care one should keep reasonably well, and indeed exceptional people keep even fitter than they do at home. The leave in Europe restores the balance and many people have managed to do very long service without ill effect. There are some people who are seldom well in Nigeria, but they are the exception, because everyone, before coming out, is put through a stiff medical examination.

Along the coast the climate is hot and damp, more damp indeed than hot. Temperatures in the year do not often run above 90°, but the dampness is excessive. During the rains mould forms on shoes overnight; and in the Cameroons bedclothes have to be put before a fire all day to get thoroughly dried. Lagos usually has a sea breeze making it bearable, but when this drops at night the closeness is suffocating.

This damp heat extends inland for some distance; but as the ground rises it diminishes and the air is just hot. In the northern half of the country life is more bearable,

5

but from December to February the wind called Harmattan comes from the desert laden with fine dust, bringing with it cold nights when three blankets are needed on the bed, and also a dryness that parches the lips, cracks the skin, and makes a smile an agony. Some people are immune to it, but most find it intolerable. Towards the end of the season and after it, the weather can be very good indeed, but in March and April it is as hot at night as in the day and sleep is often just a thing to long for. In the south there is a short period of what passes for Harmattan, but it is only a shadow of its northern self : it lasts only a few days, and makes a pleasant change after the dampness. It is marked by a haze in the air, whereas in the northern Harmattan one cannot see more than three hundred yards for dust.

The heat in the extreme north just before the Rains, that is, in May and early in June, is in the neighbourhood of 110°, and everything feels painfully hot to the touch. On opening the door of the house at mid-day one meets a blast as if from a volcano. Like poor Falstaff, one is always " larding the lean earth," and the mattress and pillow are often soaked through. The thirst is unquenchable. Once in Maiduguri, in peace-time, about thirty R.A.F. men who came over from Khartoum each drank two gallons of water in a day. We were glad it was only water, but it was quite a task to boil, filter, and cool such a quantity in the time. It is the only place where I have been wakened up by the sound of a crash in my ear caused by a drop of sweat trickling on to the ear-drum. One week-end I lost twelve pounds in weight simply through perspiring when repairing my car.

Europeans react to the Nigerian climate in many different ways : some do not seem to notice it at all, some complain unnecessarily, and some really are affected by it. Few people enjoy the shattering tornadoes that usher in the

Rains over about three unrestful weeks : the great black menacing cloud that comes swiftly from the east, the screaming wind that sweeps in from a still sky, the roar of falling rain that blots everything out and nearly drowns anyone trying to run through it, and the terrifying flashes of lightning and crashes of thunder. There are times when the ground runs with thin blue flame, the house appears to split with the thunder, and one's last hour seems to have come. But eventually the sun shines, the birds sing, and the country looks better for the rain, except for unlucky flattened crops and battered houses.

Early coasters used to say that north of Cape Blanco (near Dakar) the sun is the white man's friend. South of it they feared the sun, since death must often have been due to sunstroke and heatstroke. But recently it has been found that the sun is beneficial everywhere if there is not too much exposure to it, that some people are impervious to its rays, while others should not take the risk of being uncovered, and that its exclusion does in fact help the diseases that flourish. Dark glasses are more important than sun helmets, and light, loose clothing is better than coats and trousers. (Mungo Park wore a high " beaver," Dr. Barth a turban, Lord Lugard a pith helmet, Bourdillon a green " pork pie," and none of them suffered for it.) The odd thing is that the Africans are as much affected by the climate as the Europeans. The southern Yoruba or Ibo hates the north, shrivels visibly in the dry season, and gets pneumonia in the Rains. The northerner loathes the damp heat of the south.

Administration

Though Nigeria is called the Colony and Protectorate, no one has ever been reckless enough to try and distinguish between the two. The Governor's writ runs equally over

7

them : the departments of the Government work impartially over them both. The historical difference is that the Colony of Nigeria, consisting of a strip of sea-coast 150 miles long by 20 miles wide, descends from the old Colony of Lagos, formed after 1861, and the Protectorate is the rest, and later-acquired part, of the vast country.

The Colony is administered under a Commissioner who lives at Lagos : the Protectorate is divided very unequally into three groups of Provinces—the Eastern and the Western of very much equal area, and the Northern, which is three times the size of the two others put together. Each of these groups is administered by a Chief Commissioner who is the most senior of the Administrative staff and comes next in precedence to the Chief Secretary. Each group is divided into Provinces, under Residents, and these into Divisions, under District Officers. There are twenty-five Provinces, varying in size from 45,000 to 3,000 sq. miles, and in population from three and a half millions to half a million. There are eighty-five Divisions, at every stage of development from the pagan tribes in the north and Ibos or Kwas in the south, who need considerable external help, to the advanced Abeokuta and Kano Divisions, which largely run themselves.

Over all is the evil influence of the mosquito. It has been suggested that it was the mosquito that lost Rome her Empire : we should take no chances with ours ! The labour of control is vast, but it is not impossible with co-operative effort. Disease is the worst enemy in Nigeria. Malaria, venereal disease, the intestinal worms, leprosy and other skin troubles, yellow fever, smallpox, and oddly enough, measles (here a deadly disease), are the things that are holding back the country more than deficient education, communications, and wealth.

Early days in Nigeria : motor cycle carried over bush paths from one completed road-section to another

Kano : carriers obtaining water from a pipe-borne supply

Lagos : typical European residence in the Ikoyi Reservation

Bridge over the Niger River at Jebba

The People and the Country

As for the native peoples, no one knows how many tribes there are of them ; there are four hundred and more languages and dialects in daily use, but there are more tribes than languages. Some of the tribes are contiguous with one another and get on fairly well together, but others, though fairly close together, have mutual distrust. Indeed, there is as much rivalry and misunderstanding between the different tribes in Nigeria—and this rivalry even extends to units and groupings within the tribes—as there is between European nations, and it is impossible to obtain any concerted action when several tribes are involved, be they small like the pagan tribes of the Plateau, or big like the Yorubas and Ibos. But the country is so big that any attempt to make more than tentative generalizations is foredoomed to error : X may say one thing about a certain aspect of Nigeria and Y may say the reverse, and both may be equally right. This makes judgment very difficult for newcomers.

Nigeria is in some ways a fascinating country, but in others an exasperating one. If one takes to it, one will like it, but if one does not, one may even grow to hate it, such is its power to disenchant and wear one out. Many people come out excited and enthusiastic, but they go through the last years of their service disillusioned and disheartened. Much depends on where one starts and how one starts and whom one starts with. Little do those who welcome the newcomer realize how seriously their light and often unmeant words may affect the whole of his future career in the country. It is a fine country for the people who want to do something and to help others and who have abundant reserves of tolerance and energy, but for those who are selfish or who think that the world should revolve around them, it is the country above all to avoid.

9

There is, and will be, a vast amount to do in Nigeria, and for many years there will be jobs for the European of enthusiasm, whether under the Colonial Office or under the great merchant houses, but Nigeria is unsuitable for the settler. Children can be born in Nigeria, but it is no place for them to grow up : the sun which should be their health is their danger, and disease lurks in everything they touch. Even the adult needs to go home to Britain from time to time to recuperate.

People are apt to say that there is nothing to see in Nigeria ; they seem to mean it too. When I went out first I was told by a man who had been there a long time that there were no colours to be seen in the landscape but browns and greens ; he did not mention that there were endless tints of both, and many other colours as well. There are some very beautiful places in Nigeria, and there are some painfully dull ones, but on the whole there is a mild beauty everywhere. The rivers are often majestic and the hills have character with their twisted rocks and gnarled trees ; the plains have their great trees and graceful clouds ; the still waters of the creeks reflect the great forests around them, and the white sails of the canoes. Anyone who has travelled widely in Nigeria can readily evoke many memorable views, whether over the spacious plains or up towards the hills and mountains.

The people are amazingly interesting too. They are at all stages of dress from utter nakedness to striped trousers and black coats, and of houses from tiny mud huts perched on the rocks of steep hillsides to regular three-storey buildings. Their skill in craftsmanship, the variety of things that they can make, and their sense of pattern are remarkable. Pottery-making, woodwork, mat- and basket-making, leather and iron working, and house-building are practised in every village. Their wooden masks and figures are now well known

(446)

all over the artistic world, and their ancient bronzes and castings have a great charm. Most towns and villages are independent of their neighbours save for providing them with occasional luxuries, and could get along quite well even if they were completely cut off.

There is still much to be discovered and much to be written about, photographed, and sketched in Nigeria, and a vast amount of practical work to be done if happiness and prosperity are to be brought to that great country.

Chapter Two

GETTING ABOUT IN NIGERIA

PEOPLE have been travelling on foot about Africa for thousands of years. They have been walking or riding, carried in hammocks, or conveyed on the great rivers in canoes and boats. There is a type of European who thinks that nothing of note ever happened in Africa before the white man arrived. His frame of mind is an unfortunate one, since it creates the impression that the European not only occupied the country, but practically invented it, and that everything that did happen before he arrived—if anything did at all—was of no account. The result is naturally an undue focusing of opinion and thought on the events occurring after the arrival of the European to the neglect of those that had happened before.

" Before we came," he would say, " there was nothing but the slave trade and slave wars." These were there all right, but a vigorously complex pattern of life existed too, and the slave raiding, though it was a dreadful thing and wrought unspeakable harm to the country, could not affect every part equally or at once. In fact the places from which the raiders set out—like Kano or Ibadan—were themselves great and prosperous centres. The travel books of Clapperton and Lander in the 1820's already contain innumerable thumb-nail sketches of wayside scenes and activities, witnessing to an abundant life and the established importance of trading and the chief trade routes.

But of course there is an immensely greater amount of travel on the roads and paths of the country nowadays than ever before, and also travel is safer. In 1880 a man or a woman would not have dreamed of walking alone, say, the fifty miles between Kabba and Lokoja, though a company of five or six might have done so (Africans think little of walking long distances); thirty years later, in a single generation, no one would have thought twice about it. Now, as the Hausa says, " a virgin could carry a calabash of eggs from Kano to Sokoto (250 miles) and neither would be spoilt on the way."

Quite recently I had striking evidence of this state of security. In Bornu, which is perhaps less safe than other parts of the country, I saw a number of blind men walking along a road in Maiduguri, the Shehu's capital; there must have been a dozen of them. Struck by this I later asked the Shehu if he could account for it. He said, " Well, it's your fault, of course." I said, " What do you mean, our fault ? " And then he said, " Like this. Before your people came here blind men stayed at home. It was risky for them to travel about. Now you have made the country so safe that they can leave their villages and come and plague us here in the big towns."

The great bulk of this travelling is carried out on foot, the oldest method and still the only one that rarely lets the traveller down; and goods are mostly carried on men's heads. The weight of load that may be carried by a man in the employ of the government is laid down by law, and the distance that he can carry it is established in practice, but the same man working on his own will think nothing of carrying twice the government weight twice the usual distance for day after day.

It is almost impossible for us to realize the toughness and endurance of Nigerian carriers. These men are not, like commando troops, specially trained for a special purpose, but are ordinary men doing what to them is ordinary work. It must be admitted, however, that the endurance

13

of some tribes is not up to the level of that of others—the carriers of certain tribes have difficulty in carrying even light loads a short way, yet even among these the women are usually capable of carrying for great distances and do so cheerfully.

While the majority of Nigerians carry goods on their heads, and prefer to carry even the smallest article this way rather than with their hands, quite a number of tribes carry on their shoulders. Sometimes the women are less keen on head-porterage, partly because of elaboration of hairdressing, partly, in certain areas where the head is shaven, through superstitious fears. But most native people carry on their heads. It is odd to see children coming back from school carrying exercise books, text books, and an ink-pot on their heads. In Lagos it is no uncommon sight to see a woman carrying a rolled umbrella on her head. But perhaps the most astonishing sight is the washerman returning with a bulky bundle of laundry on his head and riding a bicycle. Since very light but large loads are apt to become a nuisance in a strong wind, loads are usually kept compact.

A man about to carry a load takes off his outer garment, rolls it into a circular pad, and puts it on his head under the load ; a professional carrier carries a special pad made of rolled-up grass covered in cloth. Women usually carry a piece of cloth which they roll up into a pad. The Hausa professional carrier has a long, light tray, curved in section and made of light palm fronds, on which he packs the load he is carrying. It will take two men to lift it on to his head, but once it is there he will go for miles without a stop.

Along all the principal routes of the north there are recognized carriers' halting places, often located by a stream or a well, and here are always to be seen either a number of trees with forked stems or a row of forked sticks standing in the ground. On to the fork the carrier puts the front of his tray and under the back of it the long staff he has been walking with. He can then step out from under the load, which is supported at each end and is ready for lifting when he wants to leave. These halting places are the gossip exchanges of the country. The women from the village bring down food to sell and hear the news from the carriers, and the carriers pick up local news from them. Other local people come in and pass the time of day.

Paths in " Trackless Africa "

People talk rather airily of " trackless Africa." There may be parts of Africa to which the description applies, but certainly West Africa is not one of them. West Africa is a mass of tracks, and was a mass of tracks long before the British entered on the scene. Mungo Park, Clapperton, and the other great explorers followed existing tracks ; they did not hack their way through forest. Every village is joined by tracks to every other village. These tracks are not very grand affairs, some of them being scarcely visible to the untrained eye, but others are trade routes, and some in the north are international caravan routes. These paths and tracks are made solely by men's feet. Sometimes a bit of tree is cut away, sometimes there is an attempt at filling in a hole, but for the most part they are just tracks on the unaltered earth.

The more important tracks are cleared to about two feet on each side of the path, and over certain streams there are very rough bridges, just boughs cut from the bush and thrown across from bank to bank. Over the largest rivers there are ferries, which have existed from time immemorial. The passage of such ferries may be made by small canoes or by substantial dug-outs, or yet again simply by floating

15

goods across in giant gourds while the passenger makes his way over as best he can—for instance by resting his stomach on a gourd while he propels himself with feet and hands (when if he is not used to it he may well slip over head-first !).

The Nigerian tracks are on the whole much more direct than might be expected ; they may wind about on the way, but their mean general direction is practically straight to the next village. If they meet with a natural obstacle they go round it, but they recover their original direction on the farther side. A track will wind round a temporary obstacle like a fallen tree or an ant-hill, and will continue to follow the detour long after the obstacle has disappeared.

Roads and Road-making

In Great Britain to-day the existence of good motor roads is taken for granted, and if roads are discussed at all it is in respect of sweeping by-passes, clover-leaf fly-overs, and the toll of injured and killed. But in the new countries of the world roads, ordinary straightforward roads, are still matters of exciting news value ; and this is particularly so in Nigeria. The war of 1914–18 found the country with no roads outside the big towns ; indeed only the Governor and a handful of important officials had cars. There were heroic journeys by His Excellency over cleared tracks, when tremendous exertions were made by all and sundry to get the car through, paths being widened and straightened, holes filled in, trees cut down and the stumps pulled out, sides of ravines hollowed out and the bottoms filled up, and causeways built across rivers. It was all temporary work, and most of it was swept away by the first rains of the new season. At times the car was hauled bodily across wide rivers, with only the roof showing above the water. But

16

such experiences proved no deterrent : the idea of motoring took hold. The great need was for the provision of roads.

People in the far north got about by buggy, and route records were kept to help travellers by stating the times usually taken from place to place, and the nature of the ground and the country traversed. Thus the time from Maiduguri to Kano by buggy, a distance of 340 miles, was about 22 days, which means that it must have been pretty hard going. Good roads were needed there too.

Sometimes on return from leave people took weeks to reach their remote stations. It was weeks before urgently wanted drugs or spares could be obtained. The mail was carried on men's heads, and not only took a weary time to arrive but frequently came to hand wet through and illegible. Roads to carry some better means of transport were urgently wanted.

When at length, after 1920, it was decided to undertake serious road-making, the first move was naturally to join up all administrative headquarters. The routes were therefore thus planned. But when it came down to the task of actually building the roads the difficulties—lack of equipment, lack of money, lack of experience—seemed well-nigh insurmountable. Nothing but the extreme urgency bore the road-builders' spirits up and enabled them to succeed.

Lack of experience did not prove the worst difficulty, because the job of road-building in Africa is largely a matter of horse-sense. Some guidance was obtained from books on military engineering—the British officials were all ex-soldiers then—and more from an excellent pamphlet prepared by Edwardes, a Resident who deserves to have his memory kept green as one of the fathers of the Nigerian transport system. Standard widths of carriage-way were fixed on and standard widths of ditch, but a good deal of controversy arose over the distance apart that carriage-way and ditch should be ; in some areas the ditch was so far away that it could not serve its purpose of draining the road and in others it was so close that anyone driving along the road was in imminent danger of falling in the ditch. But in time these things were regularized.

It was on draining, culverts, and bridges, however, that the greatest ingenuity was expended. The culverts were tunnels under the road to take the water from one side to the other before it could collect and swamp the surface.

My own working party was lucky, since our portion of Nigeria contained innumerable granite hills which tend to "peel" on the outside, leaving great boulders exposed, often near the line of the road. Granite "skin" that was flawed broke up into convenient blocks for building the foundation, floor, and walls of the culverts, while the un-flawed ones made a flat roofing over them. Thus con-structed, and sometimes cemented, the culverts were covered over with earth. If a culvert did not happen to run the whole width of the road, a pile of stones or of sticks was usually placed at each end to mark the safe part of the road. Occa-sionally the big top stones proved faulty and broke, but they rarely if ever fell in, and there were no accidents that I can remember.

In the very flat areas we had trouble trying to find which way the water would run, since we possessed no proper instruments and had to guess. There was plenty of water about, but no traceable direction of flow, and the problem was to determine whether in flood the water would flow in the one direction or the other. Sometimes the guesses proved right, at others not. At such swampy points there was no stone in the vicinity, and the culverts had to be made of wood.

Far from being professional road-makers, none of us had ever given road-making a thought before; nor could we give it our undivided attention now, because we had all our other duties to attend to as well. Often all that could be done was to set out a line, give the men some idea of what was wanted, and go on tour for a week—visiting villages, counting the people, checking up on the native courts, hearing complaints, and the like. Returning to the road-work we would inspect what had been done, mark out the culverts required—these were only put in after the line of the road had been cleared —and cope with any special drainage problem. If we did not know what kind of country lay ahead we would make inquiries about it from the headman, and work out some plan for overcoming any difficulties. Should there be hills or rivers to be negotiated we would make a full investigation, which sometimes meant spending days in the bush casting round for alternative bridge sites or swamp approaches or highland passes.

Since most of this road reconnaissance was done on foot, often through high grass, we tried to operate during the dry season, when the grass was short. Occasionally we were rewarded with a glimpse of wild animals : antelopes big and small, lions, and elephants—on one memorable trip we came across an elephants' dancing floor. Nigeria not being as rich in game as East Africa, the sight of even a few animals gives much satisfaction.

Building Bridges

Apart from culverts, bridges were the chief problem. Fixing their sites is fairly easy if it is realized that the bridge itself is the important thing ; the road can always be swung to fit the site, and so long as the deviation is not excessive it does not matter. But the stream ought to flow at right angles to the bridge and in as straight a course as possible on each side of it. Most of our earlier collapses were caused by the foundations not being firm enough, so that a scour ran under part of the stone pier.

Another difficulty not at first suspected was that since piers fill up part of the available bed of a stream they increase the speed of the current and put a greater strain on the piers themselves. We found difficulty also in discovering the high-water mark of floods at the bridge site. The local inhabitants did their best to help, and we put pegs in where they said the water-level was at flood-time. But on checking up we often found that the water in that year must have been several feet higher on one bank than on the other! The height to which these floods rose was, in fact, astonishing.

Not only does a bridge look better when raised above flood level, but also it is safer, since the pressure of a flood on the beams is very great. Some pessimists used to wire their bridge timbers together and attach them to cables secured ashore, so that timbers would not be lost when the bridge collapsed.

For these bridges we built piers of granite, and the roadway was carried on mahogany beams under mahogany planks. The span was made as short as possible, since we were doubtful of the weight that the beams would carry; about twenty feet was the normal span, but sometimes this was exceeded. The widest span I ever built was over thirty feet, but twenty-six feet beams were the longest that could be used, because it was impossible for the men to carry greater lengths than that along the roads. The general policy was to fell and cut timber near the bridge sites, but often this could not be done and the timber had to be carried on men's heads for some considerable distance. The men were highly paid for this form of labour, and there were plenty of relief workers, but nevertheless it was very strenuous.

There are few pleasanter sensations in life than that felt

when driving a car along one of your own new roads and over your own new bridges. You are anxious and critical, of course, and you discover faults that will have to be attended to before the road is really finished, but it is a grand sensation. To save time in construction, many roads had to be built in sections ; but the great day would eventually come when the sections would be joined up and you could drive for the first time over sections previously only walked or ridden on ; that, too, was a grand sensation.

Once after joining up two sections I drove my grey Morris along to the new road ahead to find that the Africans working there, never having seen a car in their lives before, were shinning up trees with amazing speed ! I had stopped the engine, got out, and eaten some sandwiches before the braver of them ventured on to the ground again. I chatted with them for some time, but the more timid ones kept pretty close to the foot of their trees, one or two even holding on to the trunk all the time. At length, when I restarted the engine, in spite of my assurances a number of them swarmed up the trees again for safety, and peered anxiously down through the branches at the weird grey object purring off along the new road.

As for our bridges, by no means all were built on granite piers, some being only slightly raised embankments (or " drifts ") across river beds, with slopes cut down to them through the banks. These were sometimes concreted over, but they did not last very long. When the rivers came down, the " drifts " were under water and so could not be used till the floods had passed. This was exasperating to travellers in a hurry, who sometimes tried to drive over the drifts if only slightly under water ; but since the edge was invisible and there was little play, it was a most alarming experience.

In some places suspension bridges were tried and were

fairly successful, but they took a good deal of building and a great deal of confidence to use. There is an African type of suspension bridge which was already in use in the country when the British arrived, and which was called locally a " tie-tie " bridge, because the vine from which it is made is called a " tie-tie." The long, vine-like tendrils that swing about from the tree tops in tropical forests are very strong, and when twisted together make substantial ropes. They are woven and hung from the branches of high trees on each side of a river, to form a great loop over the water. The track reaches them on the downward swing and then follows the arc along. The normal bridge of this kind is V-shaped in section and the footway is a bundle of small branches that goes right across the river. There is a hand-rail, as it were, on each side, but sometimes it is difficult to touch it even with extended finger-tips. The bridge swings as you cross, but it is not difficult for an unladen person to negotiate ; though how men bearing heavy loads manage— and they manage cheerfully enough—is a mystery. Only one bad " tie-tie " bridge ever came within my personal experience, and curiously enough it was regarded as a much improved type, since instead of the customary bundle of branches to tread on, there were slats across making a thirty-inch footway. In its early days no doubt it had been a triumph, but by the time I came across it one side had sagged so much as seemingly to present a sloped ladder with intermittent hand-holds. To make things worse, rain was falling heavily and the bridge was damply greasy. Yet no one fell off, or even hesitated.

Surfaces

The roads on the whole are good for motoring. From Jos to Maiduguri, one of the longest direct runs in

Nigeria, is 367 miles, which we made a practice of doing in one day. For mile after mile it was all right to drive at forty miles an hour, and though there was plenty of traffic on the road it gave no trouble, as the tall plumes of dust that arose from moving vehicles gave early warning of their approach. Unfortunately the drive was a dull one on account of the monotony of the scenery. At 138 miles out from Jos the last stone on the road is passed, the last hill has been already met with some distance back, and for the 229 miles ahead there is nothing to vary the setting but towns, villages, and occasional apologetic drops and rises.

In the north you may drive a car on a sandy camel track, where if the sand is too heavy going you turn off into the bush and drive in and out among the trees on the firm stretches : such travelling may easily take a day to do a hundred miles. To the east of this area are swamp tracks extending for a hundred miles across the southern shores of Chad : these, too, can be motored, but they are impassable for five months in the year, and have to be made up each dry season. In the rest of Nigeria the tracks are not fit for motoring purposes.

On the great road to the north-east, to Maiduguri and Fort Lamy, which carried an enormous tonnage of stores for the Allied Nations during the African campaigns, there was constant difficulty over surfacing. There were a few patches surfaced with laterite, a kind of ironstone that dries and drains quickly, but to carry the stone long distances was too expensive. We mostly used a sort of limestone agglomerate, which was fairly hard, but broke up in rain and made a fine mud ; yet it dried quickly, and having the knack of smoothing out ruts as it dried, soon became ready again for traffic. Even after very heavy rain the road would have been all right to use after a rest of twenty-four hours ; but in practice it was not possible to allow so long, and traffic was held up

23

on it for only twelve hours after the end of a rainstorm, the surface consequently suffering, though not too badly. Every twenty miles there were gates across the road with native administration messengers as gate-keepers, and there were villages nearby and rest-houses for Europeans.

Fortunately most of our road-making was in level country, but there were times when we were faced with hills. If these were gentle, the problem was easily solved, but if they were steep they could not be taken directly but had to be zigzagged or cut. If again the rock was too hard to be cut through, a system of embankmenting or terracing had to be adopted, which meant cutting a bit on one side and building up a bank on the other. In a few places quite large cuttings had to be made, and extensive embankments built. The difficulty in siting was to find the easiest gradients and to mark out the cutting and banking areas. For this we developed a simple but reliable method which consisted of pegging the centre line of the road through the bush and then tracing outwards from each peg a rough outline in sticks and rope showing the profile of the embankment to be filled up to bring the lower outside edge of the road up to the mid-level. Then as the upper inside edge was cut away, the debris was used to fill in the profile so marked out. After that the whole road width needed only a slight smoothing and surfacing. Stones removed in cutting out were used to build the containing walls for the foot of the embankment. Sometimes this cumbersome process had to be carried on for miles at a stretch, but it had its charms.

Many of the pioneer roads have now been taken over by the Public Works Department into the main network of the country. They have been modified here and there, bridges have been replaced by steel and concrete structures, drainage has been improved, and irregularities have been smoothed out ; yet the core of the seeming new road is usually the old administrative road. Indeed a few of the roads have scarcely been altered at all since they were completed by the pioneers, and to-day remain as standing memorials to human ingenuity and determination.

Digression on Railways

The Nigerian Railway, a government concern, though too often merely taken for granted, is a wonderful achievement. It possesses over 2,000 miles of track. Every other day three trains set out from the respective termini of Lagos, Kano, and Port Harcourt, to meet in Kaduna Junction, an important change-over junction. In the early evening the trains stand together against the long platform, which is a mass of roaring humanity under the dazzling arc lamps— folk rushing madly for seats, others dashing about looking for friends, the mails being tumbled out and flung into the respective trains, and mountains of luggage being transferred —till at length the chaos sorts itself out, the signal is given, and the great red trains pull out for north, south, and east, the powerful electric headlights shining down the tracks as trains hurtle through darkest Africa.

Officials on Tour

When government officials go on tour, as many of them have to do, they need to take with them all the equipment and supplies required during the whole time of absence from their stations. The goods to be conveyed are packed up in suitable " loads " which are arranged in line and allotted to the respective carriers.

Everyone has his own idea about the best method of travelling with loads. Some people walk with the carriers, trailing along at the tail of the column ; others send them far ahead, others again go on in front of them. The majority

25

perhaps send on some of the loads well ahead, so that their next camp may be ready for them on arrival. Some send the carriers ahead in the middle of the night, merely keeping a couple of men for the bedding loads. Some send on what they can at dawn, when they are woken themselves, and then follow later with the final carrier. Some again only send on the cook and his loads.

As a rule it is best to have all the carriers in front, otherwise they take their time about coming in, and one may be badly held up waiting for them. If the whole team of carriers is sent off too far ahead, misdirection is apt to occur, as it did once to me when the carriers proceeded to a place miles away from where I went myself. It took all day, and a very miserable day it was too, to get them back again.

Some people have breakfast before they leave, others have it when they arrive at the new place, and still others have it *en route*—either a picnic breakfast carried in a single box or a cooked meal prepared at the side of the road. Some of my happiest memories of the Coast are of such wayside breakfasts, both cooked and picnic. If the traveller takes his breakfast about an hour short of the end of the trek, the remainder of the staff and loads have sufficient time to reach the destination and to get unpacked and settled in before his arrival.

The carriers are usually good and get on with the journey, but naturally there are exceptions. Some are taken on freshly at each village, but others (usually professionals) go straight through. In the former case they are paid off, and then return home ; in the latter they are given enough money for their immediate needs, and the balance due to them is paid when the whole journey is completed, viz. back at the starting point. All travelling of this kind is done in country far from the motor roads, and there are still vast areas that lie so remote from them that they can only be so travelled.

26

The white official has normally a choice of means of travel. If the area is free from tsetse fly, he can go on horseback ; or he can go by bicycle or on foot. The usual distance of a day's trek is between ten and fifteen miles, which is not too far for a practised walker. In earlier days people travelled in hammocks. I used to take a hammock with me before I was used to the country, in case I should fall ill on the way, but in the end I gave up this practice. My wife used to have a hammock for the last few miles of the journey in the heat of the sun. The hammocks are either ordinary canvas ones or else chairs slung from a wooden frame covered with an awning and carried by four men. The best of these men are very good indeed and exceedingly careful.

At no time did I find walking too great a strain, though in close weather I got very hot, tired, and dirty. A bath soon put things right and then I was ready for a day's work in the new place. The paths employed varied from mere tracks in which the walker could touch the grass on either side of him, to wide trade routes beaten down by the feet of thousands : the surface varied from earth or mud to sand or rock. Some of the routes lay through swamps, and most of them crossed rivers. Many of the routes were quite shadeless, but others lay through high sunless forests or—more often—through low stunted trees of " orchard " bush. Many tracks climbed the hills, at times gradually, and not seldom nearly vertically, but the great views unfolding were worth the extra effort, and made up for many a hard day's trek through featureless plains and obscure valleys. Most of the tracks were simple matters to negotiate, but now and again a dizzy drop would require a good head.

One, I vividly remember, ran along the rim of a great rock high up on an almost vertical hillside : it was a very narrow track along the rock-ledge which was worn into foot-holds by generations of users. Far below shone the waters of a great river. The local people called it Lahira kusa, meaning " heaven is at hand," and well it might have been for those with awkward loads on a day of high wind! We had few accidents with these carriers, but on occasion a man would have the misfortune to slip and fall. The greatest calamity that could happen was the dropping of the crockery box, as that might mean making shift for many days with whatever utensils offered. There was no shop round the corner for buying replacements!

For those who like West Africa, travelling is the best part of life there. It is the way to get to know the people—whether overtaking them on the roads, or passing the time of day with them on their farms, or standing and talking about the weather and the crops to them under the trees in the middle of the village. This last is especially enjoyable if it is the old men, real ancients, their faces wrinkled and their hair and beards white, their long thin arms bare to the shoulder apart from, say, a leather bracelet charm or a knife on an armlet, their dress a blue robe open at the neck, and on their heads the remnant of what was once a white cotton cap or an old red fez. The goats and sheep wander round picking up what food they can and the women and children pass to and fro on their occupations, since everyone in a village is busy. Beneath one tree a travelling huckster opens his roll and spreads out all the little things that sell so well, cheap mirrors (really cheap—say 3d. each), flints, knives, some local cigarettes, a few matches (both these last sold singly), little piles of antimony for the eyes, and dried seeds and bits of vegetables that are certain cures for all man's ills.

The village women bring up water and wood to the rest-house under the charge of its bustling keeper. This is his big day : for months no one has come near the place and now it is overflowing with people from the great cities, people who have to be treated with respect, and who have an absurdly high standard of life. " Yes, I do remember that something was said last time about mending the roof. You think that something should have been done ; well I daresay you're right—and what's that about the boys' houses ? You wouldn't put your dog in a house like that ; well, as a matter of fact, my dog, and he's a very good one too, sleeps in just such a place. But, there, I'll see what I can do. I might be able to find a bit of matting somewhere that would help. . . ." And so it goes on. What a pity it always is that so many things go wrong on one's big day !

The keeper heaves a respectful sigh of relief as he brings up the rest-house book in the morning. Brief particulars are filled in of the visit, and the amount paid the keeper for his work and the goods he has supplied. (In the bush places the money goes to him, whereas in the big stations he is on a salary.) Rest-house books, especially the old ones, make good reading. In these days controversy and complaints in the book are discouraged, since they are a waste of time. But in the more spacious days visitors enjoyed making light-hearted remarks. In one wild place in the desert, a man who has since become a Governor solemnly wrote in the book, across several columns : " Arrived . . . intend to stay for some time." The next entry is in another hand and is dated many months later : " Above must have left : close search has not revealed any remains."

Touring by Water

In some parts of the country you can travel by water. This seems at first an attractive form of travelling, but it is slow and monotonous. All your loads are with you and there is nothing to do except sit still and be propelled. You may go in ordinary canoes, but far from resembling the kind hired by the hour in Britain, these are dug-outs forty feet long and wide enough to take a deck-chair. They are fairly steady and will carry about two tons of goods, though when thus fully loaded there is so little freeboard as to be a trifle risky. Upstream they are poled along the water's edge; only downstream do the paddles come into use.

You may also travel by barge. A barge is a long steel boat with a platform at each end for the polers and crew and the centre roofed over and divided into two—one part usually mosquito-proofed as a bedroom and the other left open as an office or sitting-room. There is a tiny kitchen at one end and a lavatory at the other, and there are side screens for letting down at night-time and in stormy weather. By barge is a good way of travelling, since you have some room to move and can eat or work at a table.

You may travel, too, by stern-wheelers, which have big single paddle-wheels and a noisy and very hot steam engine which is exceedingly apt to break down. Stern-wheelers have abundant roofed deck space, but are fair-weather craft only. Conditions in them during a tornado are sorely trying, since if moored firmly to the shore they are violent though safe, and if in mid-stream they are violent and unsafe. If the screens are up, passengers and possessions get soaked and dashed about, and if the screens are down the boat turns over (drawing, as she does, only eighteen inches). Normally travel by stern-wheeler is comfortable enough, and down-stream it is fast too. But this last is also true of other craft. I once took a week over crawling up the Gurara River in a barge, to descend the same distance and by the same means between dawn and dusk of one day.

The two advantages of water travel are that many places inaccessible by land can be reached by boat, and that the burden of constant packing and unpacking of one's things is avoided.

For a canoe trip that is really exciting "shooting the forests" on the Niger can be recommended. When the river is up it floods hundreds of square miles of forested country on either bank, and this circumstance provides plenty of hazard. At one point the road from the normal river bank to Divisional Headquarters happening to run for miles through flood-lands, a canoe had to be taken to get through the forest whenever the river was up. The current was so swift that the canoe would shoot madly in and out of the tree-trunks, dodging boughs and risking destruction every yard. So great was the surge that the water-level on the upper side of the larger tree-trunks would be as much as a foot higher than on the lower side.

So much, then, for primitive, rough travel, all of it sporting, but inclined to be slow and tiring. It was all right in the early days when there was plenty of time and not so much to do as there is now. In those days you did all you wanted to ; now you can do only what very scanty leisure permits. To-day duties are innumerable : there is a continual stream of people waiting for action on some matter or other to be taken, there are constant details that must be looked into and checked, and there are frequent visits by other officials with whom it is important to consult. Since these and other insistent calls cut seriously into the time available for touring, it is impossible nowadays to walk or boat everywhere, or even to ride ; some speedier mode of travelling has to be adopted. This is where motoring comes in.

The Joys of Touring by Motor

Touring by motor is eased by the increasing mileage of satisfactory roads in Nigeria. Roads now run in many

31

directions, and the provincial or other headquarters is unlucky that has not at least four roads converging on it. These roads cover only the main places, but they provide a quick means of reaching some point near any particular destination, after which the journey can be completed by foot, boat, horse, or other local transport. Thus it is possible to leave headquarters and get to a point fifty miles away in an hour and a half, start on the local tour (if carriers are ready and horses provided), and reach the first halt by lunch time. Thence the journey is made as before, but several days of trekking will have been saved.

To all good things there are drawbacks, and people have complained that the motor has estranged the officer from his people. When the motor is misused—that is, when the motor alone is employed—this complaint is justified, but not where motoring is combined with local touring. The only sufferers are the villages lying within a short radius of headquarters and off the motor roads, since the motor passes these by. Even in the old days villages within eight miles of a station were neglected unless they lay on the regular touring route ; nowadays the villages within forty miles are neglected unless a determined effort is made.

Touring by car or lorry is in some ways much more uncomfortable than the old ways. Unless the lorry is very large, the number of " loads " it will carry is small ; the journey is commonly dusty, hot, and tiring ; the loads get covered with dust and dirt, and the " boys " sitting at the back of the vehicle become almost unrecognizable. Serious breakdowns may occur where no help can be had, and tyres are always apt to give out—on one of my journeys in Bornu, within the distance of a hundred miles, two outer covers burst and three inner tubes disintegrated. " Disintegrated " is the right word : I looked in the cover for a tube to mend and found nothing but some red dust and a few irregular fragments of rubber.

But the African adores travelling by lorry, and will cheerfully cover enormous distances in the greatest discomfort. Even the strictest regulations against overcrowding produce not the slightest effect, nor do the appalling accidents that take place from time to time serve to check his ardour. He just climbs on to the top of a swaying heap of loads and holds tight ; he may be blinded with dust, shaken to bits, in instant danger of a violent death, but, by all that's wonderful, he is travelling !

For the official, motoring has other boons to offer besides speedy touring, especially greater accessibility to a doctor. On my first tour, before the era of motors, my wife was staying all the time at a place five days' *walk* from a doctor. Moreover the fact that one can get about and spend a week-end at a friend's house gives confidence, and removes the strain of isolation at a bush station. There is a greater interchange of ideas, from which the whole country profits.

Making the First Maps

Most of these roads were made before there were detailed maps. Mapping is a delicate and intricate business : thus the map of Britain has had a long history of development, but now it is so good that it merely needs small parties of sappers to correct it from time to time.

There are many countries, of course, where the standard of surveying is as high as in Britain. But in others with a scanty population, extensive area, and small resources the standard is lower. So it is in Nigeria.

How does one start the first map in a new country ? Does it take a long time to do ? How much can be done in a day ? Is it a difficult matter ? Or are there short cuts ? Such are the questions that are frequently asked.

Almost all governments maintain their own professional

33

Survey Departments. But professional map-making from scratch is a slow progress, and parts of the world have not been able to wait for the professionals to finish their work. A detailed Nigerian map of some kind having become a crying need, and a map with only a moderate standard of accuracy being better than none at all, the task fell to be undertaken for the most part by amateurs. The following is the method by which part of the great area of Bornu, in the north-east, was thus mapped.

Most of Bornu consisting of flat country, there is no point from which an extensive view can be obtained. The District Officer therefore did a good deal of the surveying on horseback. Mounted on his horse he would ask a local African the name and direction of the next village (and it should be noted that when an African points out a direction he is usually precisely accurate). The District Officer would take a bearing along the man's hand, and then canter on that line across country. When he reached the village he had been directed to, he would ask the people there the direction of the village that he had just come from. This they would give him, and he would again take a bearing. From the two bearings he would judge the mean direction, and from the time taken to canter from village to village he would estimate the distance (since he knew the speed of his horse). This was the method; and so from place to place in the blinding heat he rode, covering an area as big as England, plotting the details on the drawing-board in the sweltering nights while brushing impatiently from him the myriad insects drawn to his lamp from miles away, and gradually building up a map.

The amateur starting a survey for map-making normally first obtains from the Survey Department a sheet showing the positions of the " trig points " in the selected area. His own drawing from actual surveying will include these

34

points, and he adjusts his main field bearings to the correct positions; in short, he manipulates his own map by reference to the official points. This may sound an absurd and even light-hearted way of doing things, but in practice it works well enough.

But there were no official points at all for the part of Nigeria that I had to map, an area of over 2,500 sq. miles; the work on that first of maps had to be done blind. All I had was a blank sheet, and a point that I had decided to start working from.

The Art of Traversing

A traverse survey is one in which a route is mapped by taking bearings and measurements from point to point along it, and plotting these on a map. Surveying is also carried out by fixing the position of prominent points, and building up a network of triangles covering the area concerned. The methods are mutually serviceable, and a combination of the two is likely to give good results.

In traversing, the surveyor takes a bearing to the farthest point visible along a road, then walks along and measures the road up to that point and enters the particulars in his book. The stretch thus marked and measured is a "traverse." He then takes a fresh bearing, marking the angle the new stretch of road makes, and walks along it, measuring as before. So the survey goes on. Meanwhile any objects of interest or prominent elevations are noted and their bearings taken, so that when they are seen again later on, fresh bearings may be taken, and the sites fixed by the crossing of the lines on the survey map. Heights are checked by means of barometric readings taken every so often. Each day when surveying is finished the observations are embodied in a careful drawing made to a selected scale.

35

As the days go on, bearings back to fixed points will show whether the work is turning out accurate or not.

In our survey of Nigeria we had to depend on the Africans we met for information as to the names of places, streams, and prominent objects of all kinds. There was no great difficulty about this, except when it happened that two objects or localities bore the same name, when the utmost confusion was apt to ensue, and for the moment it would seem as if the map had become completely disorganized. Once in the early days of the survey in Nigeria an earnest man who was doing a traverse along about twenty miles of road asked as usual the name of the place to which each little side-path ran, only to be told the one name *gona*. In the end he made a rather superfluous note: "*Gona* must be a *very* large town." *Gona* is merely the Hausa word for "farm"!

The ideal traverse is one that "closes." Thus in theory, and if everything has gone well, the last sight when drawn will fit neatly on to the starting point or some other fixed point. In fact it rarely does. The pessimists say that if it did close exactly, it would be because the errors made had cancelled one another out on the way! On the other hand, if there is a disproportionately big error something serious must have gone wrong. But now is the chance to set the bearings right by adjusting all the last traverses just enough to even things out.

The traverses can be measured by the simple process of counting paces and multiplying by the average pace-length. Paces may vary, but there are so many other sources of error that this one may be safely disregarded. One such source of error is that traversing being of necessity often made along narrow winding bush paths, the surveyor is measuring the actual distance covered on these paths and not the direct length of each traverse, which is what must be drawn on his map. To balance up, it suffices to take off a percentage, though not always the same percentage. I have counted as many as 20,000 paces in the course of a single day, but it is exhausting work and not to be recommended.

Another mode of measuring is by using a milometer attached to a wheel. The wheel is trundled along the road, and at the end of the traverse the reading on the indicator is taken. So long as the wheel is steadily trundled the measurement is accurate, but sometimes on a rough road the man pushing the wheel is so alarmed at the prospect of damaging the wheel that he unconsciously carries it along for some distance, and the indicator fails to register the ground covered.

When traversing it is an immense gain if there happens to be a hill that can be climbed at the end of the day's traverse, since from the top a resection can be made by measuring the required angles. If a large number of traverses have been done, the general view of the country now obtained will enable the surveyor to join up the river sections —where the rivers have crossed the traverses—indicate the direction of flow, assemble the heights with confidence, insert villages freshly caught sight of but not actually visited by road, and generally obtain an adequate conception of what has hitherto seemed a hopelessly confused piece of country.

Above all, the contours can be tested. One man I knew caused wholesale confusion by entering his contours the wrong way round, so that, as Isaiah said, " Every valley shall be exalted, and every mountain and hill shall be made low." Unfortunate results can also be produced by running the contours into a spiral, an easy thing to do and exceedingly difficult to undo again. Such are the troubles of the amateur. The professional sails smoothly through when the amateur can scarcely sleep at night for worry. I have woken up at night, apparently drowning in a sea of brown contour lines twirling and twisting all over the room.

The length of the traverse depends on how much can be seen ahead. Even in open country it is often impossible to see which way the path goes, and it is necessary to have a man go on in front, but when the path runs through trees or high grass the real difficulty begins. One day I spent seven exasperating hours doing just over two miles of track, because it was very winding and ran through high grass and trees. Some quicker way of fixing angles had to be found, since there was not enough time to spare for such a slow rate of progress. After some experiments I found it—by the use of sound. I had been following the voices of the men carrying my baggage as they wound their way through the forest ahead of us. If location of the voices could have been plotted on to a map the thing would have been done much quicker. We could not in practice use voices, but we could use the next best thing—a drum. The process took some working out but the final technique had the virtue of simplicity.

The man set out with his drum, and when he had been gone about three minutes I took a compass sight on to the direction of the sound of his drum. This may sound incredible, but it is quite practicable. I blew a whistle, and the man with the drum stopped in his tracks and scratched a big cross on the road at the point where he was standing. Another whistle and he went forward again. The advantage of this system was that the length of the traverse leg could be altered merely by waiting to give the man a start (lengthening it), or by walking on a while before blowing the whistle (shortening it). Since at times the drummer could not hear the whistle, in the end we gave him a second man to walk a short distance behind him and tell him when the whistle sounded.

This method was so quick that it was possible to make good surveys at a uniform walking pace, say about three miles an hour. Using this drum method, I have surveyed ten miles of road through difficult country in three and a half hours, when by the old method it would have taken days.

The professional surveyor will say that such a survey is no good, and from his point of view it is not—it did not produce a map accurate to within a few inches. But it did give us a map of sorts, and one that we could work with, showing the shape of the land and the essential lay-out. In the fullness of time no doubt it will be replaced by a map of professional exactitude and finish, and no one will welcome that more than I. But the professional map will not be more useful to the ordinary man than ours was.

Chapter Three

FREE QUARTERS ARE PROVIDED

The Allocation of Houses

AMONGST Europeans living in tropical countries one of the commonest topics of conversation is housing. Talk ranges from the practical details of structures to the actual rights and imagined grievances of individuals who feel that they have not been allocated a good enough house for their grade, or that someone else has been granted two extra chairs and a cushion without the slightest reason. In an uncomfortable climate comfort assumes an enormous importance, maybe too much, though certainly pleasant living conditions increase efficiency and reduce ill-health and invalidism.

To some people the plans and details of buildings are always interesting, and to many others they become so if they can be talked about officiously or if there is any prospect of a practical outcome. The trouble really begins with the fact that in an African Colony " free quarters " are provided, which means that an official has no say in the matter of choosing either house or neighbourhood. It always sounds so attractive, before going out, to be getting free quarters, especially when someone you meet, very senior probably, light-heartedly presents a glowing picture of his own last house when he held some exalted position. The speaker forgets about the small house that you will in all probability get ; and so you are apt to be disillusioned on your arrival at your first free quarters. [1947 : all quarters are now rented.]

For you are a new-comer, and since human nature is much the same the world over, you will probably not get an

40

ideal house—why should you, when *somebody* has to have a poor one ? The wise thing is to be cheerful about the matter, believing that it is best to face one's troubles in one's early days, to enjoy all the more the likely good fortune later on. Besides, even as a new-comer, you *might* happen to be lucky !

Government quarters are built, furnished, and maintained by the Public Works, and the tenant is not permitted to do anything at all to his house without their consent. He can have his own bits of furniture if he wishes, and most people do have some, but the official furniture must be looked after and not just thrown into the compound. (All houses stand in *compounds* ; in West Africa the word " garden " is a verb only, the noun of it is " compound.")

Housing is an issue that brings out the greatest ill-will in man, and for the matter of that in woman too. The difficulties and worries that have arisen over the allocation of houses in Nigeria would fill a massive tome. Many of them seem very funny in retrospect, but at the time they led to grim battles, red in tooth and claw, every advantage being fully exploited and every ditch held to the bitter end. Administrators have been driven to the verge of madness over housing and its allocation even in peace-time ; in war it reached a hitherto unprecedented peak of tribulation.

When they first settled at the Coast, the European traders lived in hulks moored in the creeks. These hulks were ships with the masts taken out and an all-over thatched roof provided. Then in certain places, like Calabar and Lagos, people started living on shore, in some instances using huts of native style and construction and in others little bungalows taken out in sections from home. In time consulates were built, amazing steel and corrugated iron structures with elaborate Victorian cast-iron trimmings, in general resembling pagodas. One at least was exhibited to startled Londoners in Hyde Park. These buildings still exist and are in use in the south.

On the Gold Coast people did things on a big scale, some even living in great castles imported stone by stone from Europe. It is not easy to form a picture of what life on the Coast must have been like in those days, but despite the stone castles it must have been grim enough. There were few creature comforts, there were no white women, and even existence was precarious. Sir Richard Burton no doubt had good grounds for his description of the Consulate at Lagos—and in those days the Consuls were the rulers—" a corrugated iron morgue, which every year contained the body of a dead Consul." Fortunately, the next Government House (now the Marine Headquarters), though not extensive, showed a marked improvement on the old Consulate.

Native Built Houses

Up country, as the occupation spread slowly from the Coast, people lived in native houses, with or without improvements according to the initiative exercised. In the south, houses were of mud and thatch or wattle and thatch, and in the north of mud and thatch or just mud. The phrase " mud and thatch " is apt to suggest to the uninitiated the idea of dirt and squalor, but such is quite a wrong impression, since though some mud houses are uncomfortable and dirty, the majority are very pleasant. If properly built they are as agreeable to live in as the more elaborate Public Works houses, but they have the drawback of continually collecting dust. The dust comes mostly from the walls which, not being quite smooth, tend to disintegrate into fine particles of grit. Also the ceilings collect dirt, which falls down when the wind blows.

42

The earlier types of house were built in purely native style, with the walls sloped back, being very thick at the base (sometimes six feet and more), and tapering to two feet or so at the top. In the walls were big window openings with shutters hanging from the top and held open on sticks; but the shutters never fitted their frames properly and they let in the dust unchecked when the wind blew. White ants made havoc with the frames and often the whole shutter collapsed.

The floor was of beaten earth, or else—an improvement—of potsherds broken up and beaten into the mud. The latter made a very good kind of floor, as it was almost possible to keep it clean, and an artful selection of potsherds made a pleasant pattern. Later the floors were made of cement. This was not popular at first, for, though it made things cleaner and more comfortable, the occupier lost some of his " bush allowance," a special allowance for living in discomfort instead of in proper accommodation. The regulations were modified after a while, since the discomfort of living in unfurnished mudhouses was not reduced by a mere cement floor compared with the proper houses supplied in better stations by Government. In any event, the discomfort was not severe, but it did mean an outlay on furniture from the officer's own purse.

One of the attractive points of living in bush houses is that you can alter them, filling up a door or opening up a window as you wish. Mud work is very cheap, and after all if the next occupier does not like it he can change things back. Rooms can even be built on, and many houses have grown, by gentle accretion, from single rooms to complicated warrens.

In the far north the normal house has a flat or slightly domed roof with a low parapet through which pass pipes to carry the rain-water clear of the walls. The roofs are covered with a native cement made from the residue of the dyepits. Inside, these houses have vaulted roofs, the ribs made of mud gradually built up and slowly dried, strengthened with a cantilever of split palm trunks. Sometimes in a big room as many as four of these ribs meet from each side and cross four from the other sides, thus forming a chequered pattern on the roof. The spaces between are filled out with mud work on some kind of frame, and the whole handsomely finished with plaster and painted. Such rooms are beautifully cool, since the vaults are often as much as twenty-five feet from the floor.

When built for Europeans these houses often have a small first-floor bedroom, approached up a break-neck flight of steps with easy access to the roof, where it is said to be pleasant to sleep in the hot weather. " It is said " is used deliberately, since many people really do not like sleeping outside. It is, of course, cooler than inside, but one gets a feeling of insecurity, as there are strange noises everywhere, the moon appears in unsuspected places, and in the dawn huge birds may happen to alight on the sleeper who starts from his sleep in a terror that quite unfits him for his day's work. Then, too, dogs bark all the night and cats fight bitterly under the bed. However, many people do sleep outside, and indeed there are times in the year when sleep certainly will not be obtained anywhere else—perhaps not there either, since it may be too hot even on the roof.

Thatched roofs are very cool, and if properly made are storm-proof. In the north, grass or reeds are used ; in the south, palm leaves tied closely together. In some areas the people have a superior art in thatching, and the results are correspondingly better. But in many places it is necessary to have a new roof almost every year because of the white ants, as, in addition to the dirt, white ants and other insects are a curse in " bush houses." It is impossible to keep them

44

out of the mud work, and so they reach the roof and any timber there may be. The store, in which one keeps one's spare stuff and tinned food for a tour, is always infested with them. Even sheets of iron in the walls are ineffective against them. They have been known to come up through concrete, but probably there were pieces of wood left in it, pegs, and other things, providing the ants with both a meal and a route.

Insects

The amount of damage that the ants can do is inconceivable to those who have not experienced it. Admittedly they cannot eat iron or other metal (though they will make their way through a weak place in it) but they can and do eat practically everything else. They even seem to survive arsenicated mud. And not only do they eat things, but they build their red mud passages into and through everything, until sometimes it is hard to say what is ant's nest and what is the original article. They can live in the dark only, and they build these passages to protect themselves from the light of the sun and the attacks of birds. They make tunnels in the open too, following every leaf and twig, in a faithful but exaggerated pattern, as they eat the dead wood. They also build long thin spires straight up from the ground towards dried branches many feet above ; one can only wonder how they know that the branches are there.

The damage they have done since our occupation must run into hundreds of thousands of pounds. And it is still going on. The new houses have various ant-proof courses and other devices, but they are none of them really ant-proof. There will always be some out-of-the-way corner where the ants will get round the obstacle they cannot penetrate, or there will be some occupier who does not wage the ceaseless war required of him.

45

The main ant nests are located far underground, where lives that fearful bundle of eggs that is their queen. She is easily the most revolting of all insects : the tiny head and thorax in front of the great white bag that is just an egg-factory seems to enhance the horror of it, a living lump of fertility *in imis*. She cannot walk or move, and is protected by a sort of shell of hardened mud girt round her. She lives at the bottom of the nest. The engineer of a working party digging out ant-hills—and there were hundreds of them—on the airfield at Nguru told me that they had sometimes to go down to a depth of thirty feet to get the queen.

The depredations of the white ant form one of the biggest of the problems before Nigeria, since they affect so many of the plans for future development. Just as the mosquito injures the health so does the ant damage property. The Public Works have a party of men who go round government stations with a machine for pumping poisonous gas into ant nests wherever they find an opening. The chief effect of the gas seems to be to drive the ants into activity somewhere else, but no doubt this is a mere appearance. Anyhow it is a comfort to know that something is being done. There is a note of humour in the situation, however, since recently the forestry authorities have developed a theory that the white ant does as great service in turning over the African soil as the worm does in Europe.

Also a curious fact about white ants is that they are very seldom found in native towns or villages. The country outside the inhabited area may be thick with them, as it is in Bornu, but they are not present in the towns. Corn can be buried in pits in the ground, and will not be eaten. Some natives say that this is because in a town there is an almost perpetual reverberation underground from the footsteps of passers-by, which checks the ants in their nest-building ; perhaps the cheapest solution of the official's problem may

46

be to have crowds of people forever surging through the cloistered peace of government stations. But some cynics might say that the white ants are better.

There are other troublesome insects too, like the fascinating silver-fish, a stream-lined creature with a long thin tail, whose diet is paper, and whose joy it is to eat its way through books by beautifully tunnelled passages. Certain books contain a neat little notice inside the front cover to the effect that they have been treated with insecticide. The silver-fish appreciates this consideration very much and often gives special attention to these labels!

There is an insect that the Public Works call the " nonterrestrial termite." At first the simple thought that this meant a celestial white ant, but it is actually a wood-borer. It has turned some of the Public Works' best roofs into fine dust, and in certain places the wood has had to be taken out of roofs, doorposts and even window frames and replaced by concrete. This termite has been expensive, but not compared with the real white ant.

We must not conclude without some remarks about the cockroach. No other insect arouses such disgust in the observer, it is so revoltingly shiny and obscene, and when trodden on makes such a disgusting plop. Nevertheless I am always fascinated when watching cockroaches locating an intruder. You open the door of, say, a store and turn on the light. On the shelf may be two or three cockroaches, probably big ones. They stay absolutely still except for their antennae, which slowly wave from side to side and back to front, changing very slightly the angle between them as they do. Then they stiffen for a moment. They have fixed the intruder. Danger! Off they scuttle to safety. They do not go very fast then; they know exactly where you are. But if you chase them they move with fantastic speed, dodging in and out behind tins and if possible behind bottles, for they know, apparently, that you will not lash out at a row of bottles.

There are dozens of other kinds of insects, some harmless, others unpleasant, like the cantharides, which if alarmed raise a horrible blister on the intruder's skin—and they are apt to be much too easily alarmed. The various insect species have their seasons and their times, but most of them like a light, and if one is working late after dinner the desk is soon covered with a collection of creeping and flying creatures that would enthral any entomologist. Unfortunately, few of us being entomologists, we do not appreciate this brilliant display of Nature's fertility of resource and design. We just go on brushing away things that museums dream of, and try to keep the ink as clean as we can !

This may seem a digression, but actually all these things are just as much part of the West African house as the doors and windows.

Permanent Houses

The next phase was Government building of small concrete houses, of which the southern parts of the country got more than the northern. This disproportion has always been attributed to gross favouritism and, in general, regarded as another insult to the north, the poor fellows who live in the bush never getting a look in, and so on, and so on. Probably the real reasons were a natural tendency to improve from the Coast inland (especially noticeable when communications were still poor), a reluctance on the part of the north to press for better houses, and indecision as to the best type of house to build.

The second reason may sound odd, but I am convinced of its validity. There are two factors behind it, first the outlook of the pioneer, who thinks he is not doing his job properly if he is comfortable (when I went out first there were

48

many of these, but matrimony has effectively intervened), and second the fact that living in better houses would cost the occupier his bush allowance (a maximum of £5 a month).

The third reason, too, is important. A certain number of houses were built that might have been called " permanent," but Government, in a laudable attempt to protect itself, thought it better to call them " semi-permanent," since they did not want to spend heavily before the best patterns had been evolved, and they realized that the great variety of climates in Nigeria might make it necessary to have several types. But having built these, there was no immediate need to build better ones.

Housing Committees were set up in 1926, but unfortunately there was one for the south and one for the north, and no one seems to have thought of asking the other tropical colonies, or even the hotter European and American countries, for examples of their house plans. Instead the committees set to work from scratch as though Nigeria had been the first tropical country to design a house, but they worked hard and produced results that might certainly have been much worse. The designs adopted were far in advance of anything attempted up to that time in Nigeria, but we see now, though it sounds ungrateful to say so, that even slightly more initiative and ingenuity would have produced even better results. Among the handicaps of designing a Government house are that the plans must be of general utility, must suit the average taste and purse, and must cost no more than a pre-ordained total sum. The natural result of this last handicap, control by price, is that desirable but non-essential features may have to be sacrificed. In the more expensive houses some things can be sacrificed without loss, but in the smaller houses the slightest deprivation is serious. This is especially true of a veranda, and the veranda controversy has gone on for years and will no doubt continue to do so for many more. The indisputable points are that a veranda makes a house cooler, is relatively very expensive, and affects to some extent at least the architectural treatment and design of the exterior. Though verandas are possibly unnecessary in the cooler parts of the country, in the hotter they are almost essential.

During the war of 1914–18, when the development of united Nigeria was in its initial stages, a number of small houses were built. These were very simple and had one square room with a very wide veranda round them. One corner of the veranda was walled off as a bathroom, later other places were walled off as dressing-rooms and bedrooms, and finally the fronts were walled in as sitting-rooms. The centre, which formed a dining-room, was by this time so dark that artificial light had to be constantly in use. These houses, though lacking unity of design, were not unpleasant, and until 1926 all the houses in Kaduna, the northern capital, were of that type. In the south there was a fashion for a while to build houses on stilts to let the air circulate underneath. The houses were of wood. The design was given up, however, after a number of such houses had been built (though in brick) in Lagos.

After 1926, and the deliberations of the committees, a big change came about in housing design and materials, concrete blocks being almost universally adopted for building. New houses were now erected in many parts of the country, Jos even being planned and built as a whole on a site not previously built on.

The new houses were, as a rule, two-storied, since it had been decided that officers with about twelve years' service should have better houses than their juniors, and be able to put up guests. These houses had a sitting-room and dining-room downstairs, and upstairs two bedrooms (with bathrooms) and—in the middle, over the porch—a kind of study-cum-sitting-room : there was, too, a veranda. Such houses were very comfortable to live in, the only drawback being that a single design was imposed on all, whether at Jos, Kaduna, or the Benue Valley, when there should have been variations according to climate. For junior officers, pleasant one-storey houses were erected in the north, and two-storey ones in the south, providing all the accommodation required at that time. Unfortunately at this prosperous time not enough houses were built, the Public Works staff not being able to cope with all the work thrown on their shoulders, and the projected scheme was never carried out completely. Accordingly, in spite of high hopes entertained at the time, houses do not provide for seniority as intended, and there is a great variation in housing between different stations. The 1929 slump hit Nigeria badly, and ambitious ideas on housing had to be modified. Smaller houses were built as an economy measure, but the step has been regretted ever since.

One feature of the design of the permanent houses is particularly noticeable ; the kitchen and stores are located outside, and connected with the house by a covered passage. The purpose is to keep heat, smoke, and noise away from the house. There is a row of houses close by in the compound for the boys. These consist of single rooms, with a common cooking and sitting place, and are well built. There is also a garage (standing by itself).

The ordinary house, as previously stated, is furnished according to officially approved standards. The furniture used to be bought in the United Kingdom and sent out. It was of good quality but rather uncompromising in design. Recently there has been a change and furniture is being made locally, of local woods, and to improved designs, by African craftsmen. This furniture is of excellent quality. On the whole the supply is adequate, but there has always been a shortage of really comfortable chairs, and a total neglect of the needs of the study-sitting-room in the middle of the house. It has always seemed odd that Government has made no attempt to encourage people to work in their homes, since it is almost impossible to get a proper writing-desk out of the Public Works, and the writing-table provided is inadequate except for scribbling a few notes on.

Though there are still places with neither running water nor light, they are exceptional. Most of the larger stations have electricity, and the difference made to health and comfort by electric fans and frigidaires has been remarkable.

Every station in Nigeria contains a government reservation in which the European staff lives. Here the houses are spaced out along grid-patterned roads, mostly tree-bordered, each house set in a compound of about two acres in extent, which in a fertile region will have well-kept lawns and beautiful flowers. The reservation rarely houses commercial and native people, though there is no regulation excluding them, and there is a good deal to tempt them in. The fact is that most of them prefer to reside near their businesses. There has on occasion been considerable criticism of the so-called segregation prevailing in the reservations, yet in fact there is none, and any African caring to live by European standards can do so there if he chooses to build a house. It may be remarked that many native servants live in the compounds, whereas in other Colonies they have to remain in the native town.

The reservations are sited about a mile away from the business area as a protection against dust, noise, and infection.

Rest-houses

So much for the permanent home of the officials. Many of them, however, have to spend a large amount of time away from their headquarters; in our early days we used to average three weeks a month on tour, during which we lived in rest-houses. In some places there are "permanent rest-houses" containing furniture of a kind that no one would willingly have in his house; and nothing more remote from "rest" can be imagined. The only good point about them is that they are solidly built. In the larger stations rest-houses are built in the form of groups of rooms opening on to a common veranda with a common kitchen and a row of houses for the "boys."

The ordinary kind of rest-house is a round, thatched, mud building with a veranda, and outhouses for boys, kitchen, and latrine, and is very pleasant indeed to stay in. On a frequented route there may be two or more together, but one is usually adequate. Almost every village of any size has a rest-house, but in some parts it may be in poor condition. In Bornu, for example, most rest-houses are just grass roofs on supports, with matting round the sides, the structure seeming to be made almost entirely of white ants; and in a heavy storm part of the roof may wash down over the guests, leaving a deposit of red mud over their belongings, which will take weeks to clean. The furniture is very scanty, if any is provided at all, since you normally take with you all the things you want—tables, chairs, bed, food, and kitchen equipment as well as clothes. If you want to live in style you even take your own mats and table-cloths.

The rest-houses are set back from the roads, and some are well sited with fine views and great trees. If they are in regular use they have a caretaker, but in isolated places someone in the village is expected to look after them. For the nightly fee wood and water are provided, but all supplies for man and beast have to be paid for. Furnished rest-houses, to have staff and proper equipment, are now being built in the larger centres.

Chapter Four

LIFE IN NIGERIA

ONE never knows where to start when talking about life in Nigeria. There is such great variety in the different parts of the country that it is only too easy to give a wrong impression. Life can be very rough indeed, but on the contrary may be very comfortable, and there is every intermediate condition. Moreover, if the picture is to be painted fairly, the contrasts between European and African life must be brought out.

As for African life, the new-comer at first thinks that it is always and everywhere the same, but as he goes about the country he finds that this is quite untrue and even begins to think that the differences are extraordinary. In fact, the middle view is the right one. Compared with Europe there is much sameness set off by individual exceptions; yet there is within this general sameness quite a degree of variety.

On the Coast there is a tendency to live as close as possible to supposed European standards, but Africans have of course only the Europeans living with them to follow as examples, plus occasional and perhaps misunderstood hints from books. These Europeans are themselves living lives very different from what would be normal to them if living in Britain. Thus in places like Lagos the African houses are built to imitate British ones, and there are rows and rows of little single-storey homes comprising two or three rooms and a small kitchen with pantry and bathroom. The houses have steps before the door and little gardens. The outsides of the houses are painted in bright colours with architectural details picked out in a contrasting shade. (The bright colours, and white mouldings over doors and windows, are due to Portuguese influence and to that of returned West Indian and South American slaves.)

Some of the building estates are Government owned, the houses costing about £300 and being taken by clerks of senior and medium grade, who obtain advances of salary for their purchase. But the ordinary classes cannot afford them. As a general rule African staff, if they do not occupy Government-built houses, are expected to provide their own quarters or to pay rent. The wealthier Africans live in two-storey houses, many of which are commodious.

The African attempting to live in " European style " tends to spend extravagantly. He goes in for more ornate and elaborate household appointments than does the European in the same district. From the Government point of view the African's worst vice is ostentation, which breeds in turn extravagance and debt. When a man is in debt he is open to undue influence from others. This is why the Government takes a stern view of debt amongst its servants. Love of ostentation also prompts the buying of too many suits of clothes and the giving of an excessive number of parties ; indeed it seems well-nigh impossible for one African to admit to another that he cannot afford anything if it might conceivably lie within his means. To get it he will gladly borrow money at a grotesque rate of interest— even fifty per cent. per month is not considered out of the way. Before the war the average clerk earned from £5 to £9 a month, the greater part of which went, as a prior charge, to pay off debts already incurred, leaving so small a remnant for facing the new month that the running up of fresh debts was inevitable. The result is that in some African circles there is less disgrace in being in debt than in being free from it ! This outlook is confined to the towns, and rather to salaried workers than to others, but it is distressing. As for the moneylenders who thrive on this state of affairs, the only good thing about them is that they are not vindictive, and they give plenty of time to pay ; but, of course, in this respect time is money. The extortionate rates they charge have, unfortunately, caused a perversion of the public mind in regard to what normal interest on money should be. This we found to our cost when the Nigerian War Savings scheme was started, which offered 3d. interest on the first year for certificates costing 15s. 6d. each. The public laughed this to scorn, and only after the lapse of some time did they come to see there was any advantage in having a secure investment. The scheme has never appealed to the born gamblers, who are unhappily numerous.

The African is a keen trader, pertinacious and hardbitten in bargaining. A great deal of the trade is in the hands of women, and it is the women and girls who go to the markets. As stated earlier, the produce is carried on the head, but to-day near the bigger towns lorry services are developing.

The African is no more able to resist the temptation of tinned foods rather than home-produced foods than Europeans and Americans are. He is also apt to enjoy beer and spirits like the Westerner. In the south there is no restriction on the sale of alcoholic liquor, but in the north, a Muslim area, a permit is required, which, however, is easily procured. In the larger towns, particularly on the Coast, there are many beer shops, which consist of the ground floors of ordinary houses ; but more numerous are the palm wine booths, the wine being very heady when fermented. There are few hotels, and with some exceptions their standard is low ; indeed there is a big opening for first-class hotels, though prices would have to be reasonable for a good trade

56

to be worked up. As there are no restaurants, strangers in a town are at a loss ; most visitors, African or European, stay with friends.

Travel for Nigerians

Bicycles are becoming very popular—though women are seldom seen to ride them—and bicycle repair shops are appearing in various parts of the country. In the eastern provinces bicycles are used for carrying passengers and produce, and there are locally recognized standard charges for both classes of freight. Bicycle transport is a flourishing industry, since it seems there is hardly anything that cannot be carried by it ; and if one bicycle is not enough, two or even four may be used under one load.

Few Africans own cars, but in this respect too a change is taking place, and a tendency is arising for them to buy old crocks and nurse them along. With one of these crocks an African did a thousand-mile tour from Nigeria to various places on the Gold Coast and back, a feat that few Europeans would have succeeded in doing even with a first-class car.

In Lagos there are a number of dilapidated taxis driven by villainous-looking drivers accompanied by equally sinister accomplices. The drivers have an abandon that would be the envy of a southern European driver, yet seldom meet with serious accidents. The streets of Lagos are also brightened by a fleet of magnificent scarlet buses operated by an able and enterprising Greek. These buses are reliable and very popular, but their longest run is about six miles, from Yaba on the mainland to the heart of Lagos. Otherwise Lagos is badly provided with public transport. No doubt something will be done about it in time, but meanwhile the city continues to expand, thus providing further distances for its exhausted citizens to cover.

The vast majority of these citizens go on foot. There

are no sidewalks in Lagos, as the predilection of the town engineers has always been drainage rather than safety or comfort. Admittedly drainage is very important in a place where inches of rain may fall in an hour and where the ground has little natural slope, but it does seem a pity that the public are forced to walk in the road and are given the added handicap of a deep concrete ditch to jump when leaping for safety before an unusually erratic motor driver. The only thing that saves the Lagos citizen is the remarkable fact that they all, including children, walk straight ahead and do not hesitate as European pedestrians do. Moreover they never dart about in front of an approaching car—if they did there wold be hardly anyone left alive in Lagos. Indeed bicycles get involved in accidents more often than do pedestrians.

Colour in Clothes

Lagos displays an extraordinary mixture of clothing. The aim and ambition of everyone is to wear European clothes, but all kinds of native clothes are seen, most often the long Hausa robes, or else the Yoruba shirt worn outside a pair of shorts. The women wrap round their waists as many lengths of cloth as they can obtain, and wear a very loose kind of blouse over the top. As these cloths are always of the most brilliant colours the streets of Lagos can look extraordinarily bright and gay. Those who wear European clothes try to be very fashionable, and the young dandy is a sight to behold in his beautifully cut fawn or grey palm beach suit with coloured handkerchief, fine quality shirt, smart shoes, socks, and tie, and immaculate white sun-helmet. Wealthy business men or lawyers wear black coats and striped trousers in the best style. The women wear much the same kind of clothing as you see in an English village, though some are very smart and up-to-date. These have

58

Lagos : the Marina

Lagos : market fruit-stall selling avocado pears, grape-fruit, oranges, pineapples, etc.—always popular with Europeans, but to-day with Africans as well

" Mixed farming " : that is, the use of local cattle for ploughing and their manure for enriching the soil, a system highly approved by the Agricultural Department

their clothes made locally, usually by small tailors, from patterns found in the fashion papers ; tight-fitting dresses are preferred.

There is a big trade in cheap clothing, hats, caps, shirts, and underwear, between the United Kingdom and Nigeria, and one that is likely to grow rapidly in the future. Many quite small traders get a few dozen of these articles sent out from Britain and sell them off cheerfully for twice as much as they paid for them.

Public and Private Life in Nigeria

For amusements there are cinemas and dances. Young Lagos dances a good deal, and there are African dance bands that are excellent ; a Lagos boy made a great success as a saxophone player in London before the war. Unfortunately there is only one hall of any size in Lagos, the Glover Memorial Hall. Glover, one of Lagos's most popular governors, was a great man, and one of the most romantic figures in recent Nigerian history, but his hall is no fitting memorial, since it has a faulty design, tasteless decoration, and poor acoustics. One wonders who prepared the plans and who had the temerity to approve them. Here meetings are held with endless speechifyings, concerts and plays are given, and dances take place that sometimes go on all night— very formal affairs always boasting an M.C. and a bar.

There are three open-air cinemas. These may seem un-fitting in a tropical country, but very few shows are spoilt by rain. The spectators sit in wicker chairs and drinks are served in the interminable interval. The screen is of con-crete ; and if there are palms nearby the effect is very picturesque.

Sometimes the pictures shown are good, though they are mostly old. However, they serve to pass the time, and are popular with both Europeans and Africans. There are cheap nights for the poorer Africans. Musical shows and slapstick make the biggest appeal to African audiences.

It is amusing to watch a film when rain is streaming down the screen. The noise of the rain drowns the words and one realizes how much the technique has changed since the old silent films; one would have understood them. Frequently in fine weather lizards run hither and thither on the screen, catching insects in the high lights. How odd a glamour star looks with a lizard across her face! Up country too a few of the larger towns have cinemas, which are under the same direction as the Lagos ones and show the same films.

In Lagos there is one good bookshop, chiefly specializing in religious books and text-books; one store, too, keeps a few cheap books. Up country conditions are similar. The books on sale are mostly too expensive for the Africans, who, generally speaking, have not yet learned to read for pleasure. Though many Europeans do not seem to read much either, there is a sprinkling of well-read people. Many houses have scarcely any books in the space so thoughtfully provided for the purpose, but others have crowded bookshelves. In Lagos a very good library exists, but it is poorly patronized. In the bush the European clubs, where people do read more, have small collections of books, usually a motley variety.

In the Eastern and Western Provinces there are educated Africans who live according to European standards, but in proportion to the whole population they are very few indeed.

In general it may be said that while the older generation of educated African reflects the outlook and social standards of the end of the last century, the younger generation shows the influence of " advanced " thought, particularly Socialism, though it is more than doubtful whether this is really understood. The socialist principle fits in with the ordinary African way of life, since the general habits are simple and there is a good deal of mutual help ; but it does not appeal at all to the older and wealthier African.

In Lagos large numbers of Africans live in mere hovels ; rents are very high and native landlords callous and extortionate. Sites that in the old days were occupied by a single family have been subdivided over and over again, and now even individual rooms are being subdivided. When, about 1926, there were the beginnings of an epidemic of plague in Lagos, the Medical Department took strong measures and checked the danger in time, in the process condemning a great deal of property as unfit for human habitation. Since then there has been a steady development of slum clearance and rebuilding, with reclamation of patches of the swampy ground lying to the north of the old town. But the rate of progress has been painfully slow. The need is as great as anywhere in Europe, since the slum property and the overcrowding are if anything worse.

But there is very little money to do anything with, the Lagos Town Council spending only about £150,000 a year, drawn from rates and fees. Lagos is situated on an island which, when we took it over, had a mere fringe of houses, the rest being bush and swamp. Later when the town began to spread, the Government acquired about half of the island—the part called Ikoyi—for housing their officials. Now not only is most of the island built up, but there are as many people on the mainland as on the island—officially 120,000 people in all, but more probably in the neighbourhood of 200,000.

The simpler people are traders, labourers, and craftsmen of all types, who live very much as they did back in their native villages. They get rather more pay or profit than the corresponding people in the country, but their expenses are also greater. A cheerful and happy populace, there is a great deal of laughter in the streets of Lagos. They regard

61

themselves as at the hub of the universe, and all their friends and relations up country as very much out of things. But they still cling to their traditional festivals with drumming and dancing and the singing of their local songs.

In the Provinces

In the big towns of the Eastern and Western Provinces people live much as in Lagos, but in the villages the pattern of life is simpler, people being thrown on their own resources. The farther the district is from the railway the more this is so. In both north and south the ordinary man, even in many towns, is a farmer. He grows food not only for his family, but to sell and make a little money for the house and to pay taxes; and he may be lucky enough to get catch crops of peppers, various kinds of vegetables, tobacco, and cotton. The chief crops in the south are yams and cassava, and in the north guinea corn and millet. These are the staple foods and are eaten at all meals—most people eat twice a day only—with such additions as soups, vegetable sauces, and stewed meats. Nigeria is so rich in variety of dishes that whole books could be written about them.

The ordinary African is a villager. The villages have few amenities: no shops, post offices, public buildings, no police, and few streets; and only in some areas are schools and churches to be seen. Usually at least one road will run through a village, but if not, there will be a number of tracks converging on it. The roads or tracks will open out in the middle of the village into what may be regarded as a green, a grassy space with domestic animals at graze, and big spreading trees overhead on whose gnarled roots the goats and children scramble during the day and the elders sit and gossip in the evening.

The market, held either on the green or outside the

village in a clearing among the trees, may be an important one or may merely consist of a few stalls where cheap wares are sold and a booth or so with a treadle sewing-machine draped round with the products of it, such as caps, shirts, and shorts. (Sewing-machines are found everywhere in Nigeria, and it is no uncommon thing to see a strapping labourer walking homewards of an evening carrying one on his head, followed by the tailor, its owner. Probably no other portable machine, with the doubtful exception of the bicycle, has exerted so vast and far-reaching an influence as the treadle sewing-machine.)

The markets are the life-stream of the country, and are always popular and crowded. Moreover, in spite of their seeming confusion they are singularly orderly institutions. So that there may be no competition between markets held in the same area, it is usual for neighbouring villages to hold their markets on different days of the week. At high noon in one of the larger markets the noise is deafening, the reek staggering, the dust suffocating. The bargaining is the only thing that anyone cares about ; a tank could be driven through the throngs of bargainers without any attention being paid to it. I have known only one market to break up suddenly. I was staying in a rest-house over-looking the market from a low ridge. When the excitement was at its height I saw figures begin to steal away from the edges, then more and more made off, until there was a rush away in all directions. Sending down to find out what had happened, and thinking that a leopard must have appeared— nothing less could have had that effect, and it was doubtful whether even a leopard would have dispersed the people— I found that it was not a leopard, but the government vaccinator !

Women will walk for miles into market and think nothing of it. One day, out of curiosity I was checking the weights of loads entering a market when a very old woman tottered up with a huge load of yams on her shoulder. I stopped her to find out what weight she was carrying. It took two strong men to lift the load from her shoulders and it weighed ninety-three pounds, or half as much again as the official load for a strong man. She had come ten miles on foot that day, and after selling the yams was going to walk those ten miles back before dusk. Fearing, perhaps, that she had been forced into it by some unscrupulous relative, I asked her why she had come in with such a heavy load. She was most indignant and replied, " Why, to get the money of course."

The market installations vary widely in type. Some places have solid timber stalls, built on raised plinths, and with thatched roofs ; some have concrete or brick stalls with iron roofs ; and others have stalls, more or less in lanes, put up each time by the vendors themselves. Some market stalls look as though a puff of wind would blow them away, and others look like the wreck after the wind has passed.

To one market the women come in on horseback from miles away across sandy wastes. They dismount a couple of hundred yards from the edge of the market, and putting little sticks into the sand, attach the halters to them. The horses could free themselves with a jerk of the head but do not attempt to, standing there patiently till the afternoon when the women remount and ride back home towards the blazing sunset sky.

Some markets are highly organized. There are departments, as it were, for the different trades : the butchers are located together, the furniture men and the carpenters, the potters and the mattress-makers ; there is a corner for firewood and for enamel ware ; there are lines of tailors where the machines hum, and streets of leather workers, their stalls gay with brilliant but unfortunately unstable colours ; there is a corner for corn-dealers and Fulani women with great

64

bowls of milk, another for mat-sellers, and still another for the assorted smallwares men. On the edge of the market lie some circles of ash. Bright fires burn on them and round the fires are " fences " of skewered gobbets of meat stuck in the ash and grilling. The smell from these compensates to some extent for the other odours of the market, and I have often even wondered whether I might not for once risk tasting these delectable morsels—but never have done so.

The Village

The villages are made up of huts which are in turn grouped into " compounds." The huts are in some places round and in others rectangular in plan. Almost all are thatched in the material most readily available; in the north and middle chiefly grass, in the south, mats of palm leaves. In some places the huts have mud ceilings carried on crosssticks, which keep out leaks and render the houses fireproof.

The nature of the material used for the roof frame determines the size of the building. Thus with strong uprights a wide span can be maintained, the roof being safely carried on the uprights, but where little timber is available the span must be small, as in parts of Bornu where the roof frame to take the thatch may merely consist of withies woven into a shallow basket, which is supported upside down on the walls. In the extreme north the houses have flat roofs. Whatever the material of which it is made the ordinary native hut costs very little indeed, perhaps a few shillings, often the whole structure being made by the family themselves with a certain amount of help from friends. But in the large towns houses vary more, and there are professional builders.

In the south the people live in rectangular huts with doors and shuttered windows. Each hut may contain three or four small rooms with a common doorway into the street, and at the back a kind of yard with a kitchen, outhouses, and a few pawpaw trees. In the north the huts, which are single-roomed (one for each man and woman), have an open space between them, but are enclosed as by an outside wall with thick matting or mud walling. There is only one entrance, which is through a two-doored hut into the lane outside. This hut forms the reception room of the compound, where the master sits and talks to callers and eats his meals. All traffic in and out passes through it, but it can be shut at night so that the family may feel secure within.

The chiefs' houses are much the same, only they are larger and often so full of huts and corridors as to form a veritable maze. In the huts there is little that can be called furniture : a bed of hard mud or of wood, a few mats, some cooking pots, a big wooden mortar for pounding grain, and perhaps one or two small stools. There are often, too, several rough implements like axes and hoes, a bow and quiver of arrows (hanging on the wall), and a spear (stuck into the thatch). The interior of the hut is black with smoke, but that helps to keep the insects under control. No one seems to mind smoke. Once when I was smoking a ham the gardener craved the honour of having it done in his hut; it meant that I should be paying for his fire, and he did not worry about the smoke.

In the villages there are no amusements in the European sense of the term, yet life is by no means dull, and the people are happy and contented. There is sometimes dancing in circles in the moonlight, there are local drummers and pipers (who are farmers as well), and from time to time there may be visits from wandering story-tellers or singers who recite verses impromptu, friendly or sarcastic in tone according to the generosity or meanness of their reception. Sometimes, too, half-tamed hyenas may be brought to the village by showmen, but though these attract crowds of people, they

66

do not seem to perform any noteworthy feats. Funerals and weddings are always great events, with accompanying drumming, dancing, and professional singing ; and except in the strict Muslim areas a good measure of home-brewed ale disappears down thirsty throats. After all, weddings and funerals are beloved the world over.

The children help in the house and on the farm. They play games with mud, or from the pith of guinea corn they mould cars, lorries, and aeroplanes ; but they do not learn to regard playing as an art as children do in Britain. Playing is just something they turn to when they are not busy with a set job.

The Life of Officials

The life of the European in Nigeria is nothing like what popular imagination or the fertile invention of ignorant and untravelled authors has represented it as being. It is a steady life of work and recreation. The men are busy at their duties in the day-time, they return home for a hurried lunch, get a little sleep, and go back to the office. In the mornings the women attend to household affairs or sit and read or sew or pay visits, and in the afternoons they rest, and then perhaps join their friends about five for a game of tennis or golf, or for a walk until the hour of sunset. It is an unsensational life.

In Lagos on Sundays people often go to the beach, where there are huts to shelter in at mid-day. In the big stations [1] there is a good deal of entertaining either for a drink before dinner-time or at dinner itself. It is now the thing to ask people in for an early dinner and then go to the cinema. Sometimes parties go on to dances at the

[1] Lagos has about 1200 Europeans (to 200,000 Africans), Ibadan 150 (to 320,000), Kano 120 (to 100,000), Enugu 100 (to 75,000), Maiduguri 25 (to 40,000), Bauchi 12 (to 20,000).

Club, and sometimes they play party card games in their own houses. Occasionally an active hostess will set to and devise an evening of nerve-racking strain for her guests, in which they find themselves solving puzzles, searching for the unfindable, smelling queer things, and engaging in breathless competitions until in the end they discover that they have had the evening of their lives.

On the whole, in spite of popular opinion to the contrary, Europeans keep fairly healthy in Nigeria. There are some who are constantly ill and others who tend to break up after a certain time on each tour, but the general standard of health is satisfactory, especially when compared with that of the African, which is deplorably low. People are smart to look at and interesting to talk to. " White Cargo " does not exist here, and though there are occasional scandals, life proceeds on the even tenor of its way.

In a large station there are many hobbies and interests, and people can have plenty to do outside their official work. But in small stations there is little to do and less to talk about. The worst station is the kind that has about seven or eight people, who are inevitably thrown together too much. If there happen to be incompatible people among them, one fine day, of course, civility will fail, and there will break out one of the classic rows that are followed with the closest interest by all the neighbouring Provinces. Everyone takes sides with an intensity worthy of a sectarian movement until one of the protagonists is moved away and the storm dies down. In a large station one can choose one's own friends and, though it is politic to associate fairly closely with one's colleagues, outside contacts can also be made.

Except for Headquarters office staff, who get away only occasionally, most officials spend a good deal of their time on tour, there are so many things and places to inspect.

68

Although touring is often uncomfortable, there is always a certain element of adventure about it, too. The greatest degree of comfort on tour is enjoyed by the railway officials, who travel in a self-contained coach on the main line, the coach being taken off the train at the desired station and put into a siding, ready to be taken on in due course to the next place.

Most stations nowadays have at least one club. Clubs vary from the important ones in Lagos or Enugu to quite unpretentious ones in the bush stations, and in all of them games are played, whether only darts, cards, and billiards or elaborate team games like polo. There are the usual amenities—a small library, a lounge, a wireless set, and a bar. There may be a room for a good dance. The Ikoyi club even boasts a sprung dance floor which is a joy to the feet—and a spacious dining-room. At Lagos the grass courts of the tennis club are of first-class quality.

The tin-mine area on the Plateau is of a different character from the rest of Nigeria. In peace-time there were about 700 Europeans living within 50 miles of Jos, the headquarters of Plateau Province and more or less the centre of the mine-field. Some of the white miners and many members of the mines staff have lived out there happily for a considerable number of years without a break, for the high altitude makes the climate healthy. Some people have even returned there, building themselves agreeable houses of simple materials and surrounding them with beautiful gardens. Almost anything will grow on the Plateau and practically every species of plant has been tried. The Plateau people live in luxury compared with those in other parts of Nigeria, and their hospitality puts the rest to shame.

Chapter Five

THE COUNTRY AND ITS PEOPLE

SINCE Nigeria runs from the coast inland towards the mass
of the African continent, and for a large part of its breadth
mounts steadily in height, the country shows a succession
of belts of different types of vegetation. This effect is
reinforced by the distribution of rainfall, which is heaviest
on the coast and gradually diminishes inland, the sixty to
seventy inches a year at Lagos dwindling in Bornu to
twenty-five inches. But there is one striking exception,
namely, in the direction of the Cameroon Mountain, where
at one unhappy point the fall is over 360 inches.

The Niger Delta and its Hinterland

Midway along the coast of Nigeria lies the vast Niger
Delta, a network of twisting creeks of endless variety, from
those so narrow that they will not take any craft but a small
canoe to others, like lakes, that will comfortably take ocean-
going steamers. At Port Harcourt, on the eastern side of
the Delta, one is apt to be incredulous at the sight of a
large mail steamer moored against the wharf in a stretch of
water seeming to possess no means of exit, mangroves
appearing everywhere to close it in ; but the sight is decep-
tive, since there is actually good ingress and egress. The
waterways are very intricate and misleading, but to-day the
main channels have all been charted.

In the creeks dwell considerable numbers of people, their
houses as often as not perched on stilts, there being little dry
land to build on, just a sandbank or so here and there. The

whole area is thick with the dark mangroves, which though unbeautiful trees have many uses, the trunks yielding strong timbers for wharfages, and the branches when burnt an ash from which salt can be extracted, a product that proved important during the Nigerian salt shortage.

The water area continues on each side of the Delta proper, fanning out into lagoons running roughly parallel with the coast, so that the journey of about four hundred miles from Lagos, or even from French territory farther west, to Calabar on the east, can be made by launch without once going out into the open sea.

Immediately north of the Delta area lies high forest, the real tropical forest of the story books, the trees soaring high into the air, myriads of creepers dangling from their tops, and the ground beneath hidden in a tangle of undergrowth so dense that it is almost impossible for a walker to turn off the narrow tracks except at the clearings, where the villages and farms are. The forest yields splendid timber for building and lovely figured woods for furniture-making, but only on its outskirts do the palms grow that produce the oil for export. Many different kinds of palms are grown in Nigeria, the most important being the oil palm. Then there is the raffia palm, whose centre rib is used for many jobs about the house, the coconut palm with its smooth trunk, the palm from which mats are made (in the north), and the fan palm with enormous circular leaves. The fan and the coconut are the only really beautiful species of palms.

Lagos

At the western end of the Nigerian coast stands Lagos the capital, a picturesque town largely built on a sandy island lying in a lagoon, whence arose the name " Lagos." Seen from the sea, as the ship makes past the long moles that stretch a mile out into deep water, the white houses of Lagos look very attractive, with their green lawns sloping down to the blue water. There are coconut palms, many other fine trees, and numerous variegated shrubs on the Marina, the road running much of the way along the water-front, which ends at the Customs Wharf. Behind this last rise the closely packed houses of the African town, while across the water lies the Apapa Wharf, started about twenty years ago and not yet completed.

From Lagos the railway starts on its 750-mile run to Kano on the fringes of the desert, but the railway station is to the north, on Iddo Island, which is joined to Lagos by a bridge. Across another narrow strip of water, and lying on the mainland, is a big and rapidly developing extension of Lagos, where are situated the workshops for making railway engines and rolling stock. Here, too, is the Yaba College.

The Interior : Western Nigeria

In the forests farther north are cocoa farms, all native-owned and tilled. Until about 1920 the cocoa industry did not exist. Then planting started on the Gold Coast, and seed was sent over to Nigeria where the trees spread and the industry developed until now the two colonies grow half the world's supply of cocoa.

The Rain Forest gradually thins out through an area of " orchard bush," inland, until wooded country is only found along the courses of rivers and streams. For thousands of square miles the country is covered with this bush, and resembles an irregular orchard of stunted trees, which however do not bear any fruit. The grass here is high, say about ten feet at the highest, and is very difficult to penetrate off the tracks. In the dry season it withers away and is burnt by great fires that eat their way over hills and vales. Then the country becomes undulating, granite hills here and there rising above the trees, sometimes with fine views from the summits. Some of the hills are as round as a dome and as smooth, and others are rugged and broken ; trees grow out of the crevices in the rocks and baboons and rock rabbits live about them.

The Yoruba people live in the area of forest and orchard bush lying west of the Niger. They tend to live in large towns, and one of them, Ibadan, is the largest true African town (that is, excluding Cairo and Johannesburg, which are not comparable). Since it is fashionable for the houses to have corrugated iron roofs, which are rarely painted and mostly rusty, the appearance of the towns is far from attractive. It is not everyone that can afford corrugated iron, but unfortunately most people can acquire old petrol tins beaten out flat, which they use instead. When these are new they glitter in the sun with the greatest splendour, but their day is a short one, and before long they become rusty and dilapidated. To make matters worse, since they are attached to roof frames constructed of ordinary untrimmed sticks— what the Coast calls " bush sticks "—extreme irregularity of outline prevails. The general result is deplorable, and when there are hundreds of acres of such buildings, any hope of future improvement seems remote.

The towns sprawl over the hills like great rusty-coloured carpets speckled with green. Though there are some attempts at imposing public buildings, they are mostly of heavy and poor design. The best that can be said of them is that they answer their immediate purpose, which is to keep out the weather and shelter a reasonable number of persons more or less adequately.

The Yorubas, a race with a long and eventful history handed down verbally, are a very industrious and intelligent people, noisy and argumentative by European standards,

73

but they make good farmers, keen traders, and excellent craftsmen both at their ancient industries and at the new ones they have learnt from the British. Their weaving of native cotton is excellent and their pottery reaches a high standard. At Ife in the heart of Yorubaland there is a chief who is the religious leader of most of the country south of the Niger, and it is there that bronze heads have been unearthed of an art so admirable as to have achieved a reputation far beyond Nigeria. Their workmanship is fine, their expressions are serene. Various dates have been attributed to them, but none more recent than the fifteenth century A.D.

The Yorubas appear to have come into the country they now occupy as almost the first wave of those great tribal influxes that brought most of its present native peoples to Nigeria. If this is so they must have been in the land for at least a thousand years. Though they are so different, legend makes them akin to the Hausas. It surprises most Europeans in Nigeria to learn that these peoples have any history. There is an impression abroad that there was none before the white man came. The fact is, of course, that many great negro kingdoms existed, and that like European dynasties they had their ups and downs, and from time to time produced their heroes, their monsters, and their poltroons. Some of these kingdoms were of vast extent and influence, and others were small chiefdoms rising for a moment to eminence, only to sink back into decay and memories.

The later Yoruba history consists mostly of a grim series of internal wars between different towns and localities, deadly struggles on a strictly commercial basis. Their object was not self-preservation or victory, but slaves. Countless people perished in these wars, and all the prisoners (on both sides) were sold into slavery. Not for nothing is the Coast of Lagos called the Slave Coast; hundreds of thousands of

74

A Hausa hunter : on his shoulder a bow and narrow-bladed axe ; on his chest and in his cap, amulets containing verses from the Koran

Ife : two of the ancient bronze heads found in the district

Yoruba dancer and drummers : thorn-wood figures carved by
Mr. J. D. Akeredolu, of Owo

captives, over the years several millions, plodded along the roads to the Coast. Those surviving the horrors of the journey were sold to European dealers, and awaited the dreaded ships that were to take them away for ever. For every slave to reach the Coast probably one person was killed in the action preceding the capture, or else died on the journey. For sheer horror there is little to equal it in the period between Genghis Khan and 1940.

Resolved to stop the Nigerian slave trade, the British in 1851 made a daring attack on Lagos Island, an attack that hung in the balance for most of one stifling Boxing Day while the British ships grounded and were bombarded by the batteries along what is now the Marina. A treaty was made but not adhered to, so that in 1861 the British were compelled, in order to stop the trade effectively, to occupy Lagos. The occupation of the rest of the country came about in like manner.

South-east of the Yoruba country, in the high forest, lies Benin. It was here, in 1897, that the early administrators met with a great calamity. Compared with some modern incidents it may seem insignificant, but at the time it struck dismay into the whole civilized world. Since human sacrifice on a large scale, with slavery and every species of brutality, persisted in Benin, Acting Consul-General Philips remonstrated with the Oba of Benin, and then decided to pay him a friendly visit with eight other Europeans—that was most of those available. He landed near Benin and set off on foot for the city, the way lying through thick forest. With the party were two African clerks and 230 servants and porters. At 4 p.m. men suddenly started shooting at them from the undergrowth beside the narrow path, and one by one they fell. They were quite unarmed and Philips's last recorded utterance was " No revolvers, gentlemen, please." There were only two survivors of the whole party, and one of these was badly wounded. A naval force had then to be sent to Benin, and their description of what they found in the city further horrified the world.

Though many of the splendid art treasures of Benin were destroyed in the fire that swept the town, and others were carried off to Europe, a number still remain there, as for instance a group of bronze figures of Obas and Portuguese men-at-arms dressed in sixteenth-century armour. A museum is being built to preserve them permanently.

Benin to-day is a model town with an excellent administration under an educated and progressive Oba ; but the old court ceremonies still continue, and on state occasions the ancient coral dresses are worn.

Eastern Nigeria

To the east of the Niger the country is similar, with high forest and palm trees, but it passes farther north into open country resembling downland, with attractive hills and valleys. Enugu, the capital of the east, is a beautiful station situated on these downs. Here coal outcropped, and working began before the last war. To handle this coal traffic Port Harcourt rose out of the swamps of the Delta and the Eastern Line of the Railway was started. Nigeria used to import coal, but now has enough for herself and also to export along the coast. The coal is not of the best quality, but it can be used for locomotives.

The Enugu Government buildings are in good red brick, and they stand out among the modern products of the Public Works for their grace of line and excellence of construction. The Chief Commissioner lives in a charming house finely situated above the river. The roads have neat curves and none of the stiff formality of some of the other towns. Enugu planning, though not among the most modern achievements, shows what results can be obtained from intelligent enterprise.

To the south of Enugu there is high forest, with creeks and rivers of the clearest water ; to the north, open downland, pleasant country.

Around Enugu live the peoples of the Ibo tribe, with a total population of some three or four millions. When driving along the network of roads in the area, one seems to be going through one endless village, so closely do the dwellings follow after one another, for the population is relatively dense. Further south, round Calabar, are Ibibios and Efiks, who have some tribal legends but no known history. In appearance they differ from the other peoples, being sturdier and stockier, but they are equally intelligent. They have no central tribal organization, and seldom even group their villages. Their geographical position suggests that they possibly came into Nigeria even earlier than the Yorubas and Hausas.

Well to the east, on the coast, which continues to be a maze of creeks, lies Calabar, once the seat of the Consuls-General who ruled the Oil Rivers (as that part was so picturesquely called), now a Provincial Headquarters of a go-ahead people. Behind the swamps in the dense forest are masses of wild rubber trees, and then the foothills of the Cameroons massif. Further east still is the Cameroons Province, a rugged mass of hills sweeping up to the 13,370 ft. Cameroon Mountain itself that abuts on to the sea and faces across the straits the sister peak of Mount Clarence (9,369 ft.) on the Spanish island of Fernando Po. The Cameroons were German (*Kamerun*) in 1914 ; now the British Resident lives in the *Schloss* of the German Governor. Nigeria administers two-ninths of the old Kamerun under British Mandate ; the French hold the other seven-ninths in the same way.

77

Right across the map of Nigeria runs a great water line. The Niger comes in from the west, and as it turns to the south the River Benue comes from the east to join it. The Benue is not a long river like the Niger, and does not figure in those fascinating lists of the world's longest rivers (the Niger is the tenth, with 2,600 miles), but it is sufficiently large to carry the dignity of an " international waterway " and a million pound road-railway bridge at Makurdi. It is a wide and deep river, and when it floods, as it does once a year for three months, large river steamers can reach Yola, 800 miles from the sea. Yola is the headquarters of a largely Fulani population.

The Parkland of the North

The northern slopes of the two rivers are much alike and are covered with orchard bush. The ground rises more rapidly than it does farther south, and in a hundred and fifty miles is 2,000 feet above sea-level on the Niger side and over 5,000 on the Benue side. To the west the country is still comparatively flat, with granite hills here and there, but the orchard bush has gone and there are great trees standing at intervals, so that this country is spoken of as " parkland." It is lovely in a quiet way. Herds of white and brown cattle graze on the short herbage, undisturbed by the white egrets in their midst ; there are sturdy goats and flop-eared sheep ; the villages have neatly thatched houses ; and in the distance loom ranges of hills, rugged and grand. Nearer at hand are bare granite peaks jutting up through the varied greens of the trees at their bases. This is the southern edge of the huge area occupied by the peoples whose mother tongue is Hausa.

In this rolling parkland stand Kaduna and Zaria, the first the capital of the north and the second the seat of one of the great Emirates, founded five hundred years ago by

78

one of the few women figuring in Nigerian history. Kaduna was built in 1916; it is entirely new, and has no native associations, since it is situated in one of the areas devastated by the northern slave trade. It is quite a pleasant place with plenty of space about it. Unfortunately its first buildings were put up during the war of 1914–18, and the standard of architecture is not good: moreover it was laid out rather too faithfully on the grid system. But each road is planted with a different kind of tree, and at almost any time of the year the trees lining one of the roads will be in bloom. At Kaduna live the Chief Commissioner and the Commandant of the Nigeria Regiment, whose 1st Battalion is located here. The personnel of the technical departments in the Northern Provinces also have their headquarters in Kaduna. In a great curve to the east and south runs the Kaduna River, a majestic mass of water pouring over the rocky barriers. The climate at Kaduna, seldom too hot or too cold, is the best in the whole country.

The Plateau

Farther east the ground rises up to the high country around Jos. The tin-mines are centred on this town and cover most of the Plateau (as it is called). This is short-grassed, treeless downland over 4,000 feet above sea-level, and to the east of Jos, and not far from it, rise jagged heights to well over 5,000 feet. The Plateau is country with fine rolling outlines, and from the edge of it there are views across the plains far into the blue distance. The Plateau is occupied by tribes the Europeans dub " pagans." This does not reflect on their religious beliefs particularly, since these do not differ very much from those of people off the Plateau. But it indicates that they tend to go without clothes.

The men wear leather aprons, if anything at all; the women have a variety of exiguous costumes, the basis of

79

most of them being a bunch of leaves, sometimes front and back and sometimes only in front. But there is a great variety of other effects, varying from bunches of iron chains to strings of cowries, a single blue stone, or a single strand of string. The women of one tribe even affect a flowing tail made of white tree-fibre. The Plateau peoples (their tribal names are too numerous to mention) are believed to be the original inhabitants of the country, and they occur in a great belt from a point near Minna (south of Kaduna) to the hills round Yola and farther north. The tribes differ considerably, but scantiness of costume is universal among them, and seems to reflect a common origin.

The Far North

To the north again the country sinks gradually towards the Sahara. The landscape is still predominantly parkland, but thin acacias, the thorn trees of the desert, begin to appear. At length the level is reached, and for thousands of square miles round Lake Chad the country looks as flat as a table, a thousand feet above sea-level though it is. The people here are all Muslims and wear many coverings ; the men, bearded and dignified, have ample flowing robes of native woven cloth, the women have lengths of cloth wound about them. The women, garbed in blue or dark red, walk with grace, but their scarlet teeth (stained with tobacco flower) seem to the Western eye a disfigurement. They are the Kanuri and Shuwa Arabs of Bornu.

Across this huge area the Fulani wander with their cattle : they have been wandering for perhaps three thousand years. They are a fine race: slim, straight-nosed, and straight-haired, with skin of a copper colour. They are a mystery people, since no one knows whence they came. Many theories have been advanced, some people even saying that they are the Philistines of the Bible. They have travelled all the north and west of Africa, driving their splendid humped cattle from grazing ground to grazing ground, and are still moving on to-day.

From west to east lie the three great Hausa Emirates (principalities) of Sokoto, Katsina, and Kano, followed by eight smaller ones, and last, in the east over against Lake Chad, the Emirate of Bornu.

The Hausas and the Bornu peoples came into Nigeria about the same time, a thousand years ago or more. Kano has throughout been a centre of trade, Katsina for centuries was a seat of learning, and Bornu was known to the Mediterranean countries from about the twelfth century onward as a central African kingdom. The Bornu people, whose origin is obscure, are not akin to the Hausas; indeed they are believed to have been for many hundreds of years suzerains of Hausaland. Their great rival was Kano, but often there was a struggle with the Hausa states as a whole.

The Hausa peoples accepted Islam in the fourteenth century; Bornu had done so three hundred years earlier. Throughout the intermediate period they were fighting each other, sometimes one gaining the upper hand, sometimes the other. There were also incidental wars with other states: Katsina fought Kano, and so did Zaria; and a great series of raids over a period of a hundred years brought the Jukons of the Benue valley to the fringes of the desert. The Hausas fought the Songhai of Melle, and at one time came into conflict with the Moroccans, who overthrew the great kingdom of Timbuctu.

As time went on, the religious zeal of the people fell away, and at the beginning of the nineteenth century it must have been at a low ebb. Taking a grave view of the decline a Fulani called Usuman dan Fodio, who lived in the Sokoto area (before Sokoto was built) started a revival

81

movement. He was a powerful preacher and a man of devout life. Gathering a number of adherents, he put pressure on the local indigenous chief, Yunfa. The pressure being resisted, open war developed and in time swept right across Hausaland. Yunfa wrote piteously to his neighbour ruler: " I ignored a small fire in my country and, lo, it has grown and burnt me up." In Nigerian history this is called the Fulani Rising, and by the Moslems a Jihad or Holy War.

After ten years or so of fighting the old chiefs were thrown out of the principal places in Hausaland and the throne of Bornu had been seriously threatened. Then from the east another holy man appeared and delivered Bornu from the Fulani. It is difficult to say how serious the fighting was, but a description of one scene of the war by an eye-witness, Captain Clapperton, R.N., suggests that it may not have been very fanatical. However, another account, of a little earlier date, by Major Denham, of a slave-raid south-east of Bornu, reflects a more formidable struggle. The truth probably lies between the two. There is no evidence that these wars were waged on behalf of the slave trade, but a good deal to show the motive as religious, certainly so far as the leaders were concerned. Perhaps the followers were not so high-minded.

The result of this war was that the whole north from the Desert to the Niger and the Benue, except for Bornu, became ruled by Fulani chiefs, deriving authority from the Sultan of Sokoto (as Dan Fodio's son called himself), who had founded and built a new town of that name in the plains by a big tributary of the Niger. Sokoto is now the centre of a dense population. The Fulani who live in the towns and who have given up their cattle-herding are almost indistinguishable from the ordinary Negro types, though they are still proud of their Fulani blood.

The Fulani chiefs, some of whom were uncommonly

capable and far-seeing men, possessed certain elementary conceptions of organization and government : they had a system of district administration, they held courts of justice, and they established trade through the institution of regular markets. But once in power they went in openly for slave raiding, and the small unattached tribes round the larger Emirates soon found themselves in danger—where there were hills at hand they had some chance of fleeing, but in the plains it was almost impossible to escape the clouds of horsemen that swept the country in their gay finery. The Plateau pagans were forced to retire to their fastnesses, where they fortified the high, dry stone-walled lanes approaching their villages with thick hedges of cactus ; a horseman unfortunate enough to break into a village would have much to regret before he got out again.

This slave-raiding was not a new practice ; the old chiefs had gone in for it sporadically before, but the new Fulani brooms swept the country quite clean. The traffic was continental and not coastwise ; some of the survivors were used by the victors as slaves and some were exported across the deserts to far distant places. The losses among these must have been cruel in the extreme, for the journeys were appalling. One needs to distinguish two distinct slave trades : one in European hands, along the Coast, feeding the markets of the Americas, the other in African hands, in the interior, supplying the Mediterranean and the Middle East. The first was eventually stopped, after negotiation among the Powers and active control, but the other could be stopped by actual occupation alone.

European Exploration

The first Europeans to land in what is now Nigeria were the Portuguese in 1472. They did some trading along the Coast, but after a while their influence yielded place to that

83

of the British. There was no penetration inland until comparatively recent times, and oddly enough it came from the north and west and not from the sea.

At the end of the eighteenth century the chief African problem occupying the minds of those interested in geography was as to the course and outlet to the sea of the Niger. Several attempts were made to explore the river from the west, the best known being the two expeditions of the Scots doctor, Mungo Park, both starting from the Gambia. On the first he travelled alone across a large part of what is now French West Africa and penetrated to the Niger. On the second, a more organized attempt, in 1805, after reaching the river he attempted to travel down its course in a canoe. He had about fifty white people with him when he started out, but all save four had died before he even set sail on the river. Eventually he and the remainder were drowned in the Bussa rapids (though this was not established till twenty years later) and geography did not profit from this journey.

After that attempts were made from Tripoli across the desert. Clapperton led the first of these, reaching Bornu, Kano, and Sokoto, and returning safely; but the secret of the Niger was still undiscovered. Leading a second expedition from the coast near Lagos, Clapperton crossed the lower Niger at a point not hitherto reached, and went on to Kano and Sokoto; this was in 1826. At Sokoto Clapperton died, but Lander, his valet and sole survivor, got back to the coast after many adventures, and then, inspired by his master's enthusiasm, went out a second time with his brother. This expedition succeeded. After long delays they got a canoe at Bussa, where they heard the story of the death of Mungo Park, and travelled down the Niger. In November 1830 they reached the sea in the Bight of Benin, and the Niger riddle was solved.

84

The Navy then took the job over. In 1841 a strong expedition, employing the first steamers built for the Navy, went up the river, making treaties with chiefs as they went. They got about four hundred miles up the great stream when sickness forced them back. It was this expedition that gave the coast the name of the White Man's Grave, for losses were serious, a third of the men dying on the river, and another third being invalided for life. Still further expeditions were undertaken both up the river and from Tripoli. Many books written by those who took part in these explorations still make fascinating reading.

The Royal Niger Company and After

The Royal Niger Company, as it was eventually called, then started trading on the river, and later was granted a charter to administer the area that it had covered. Meanwhile the Foreign Office tried, rather reluctantly, to run the coastal area. Some degree of penetration became necessary to stop the slave trade wars that were going on all the time, and stage by stage the whole of what was to become Southern Nigeria fell under control, and was put under the care of the Colonial Office. There was very little actual fighting in all this : a shell from Bower's battery finished the Yorubas at Oyo ; four of H.M. ships were needed against Nana, a vigorous piratical chief in the creeks ; a column had a brief but decisive fight against people north of Calabar who were running witchcraft in a big way with a fine slave-dealing business ; and there was a stern little fight before the Ijebus agreed to allow free trade.

This does not mean that there were not other incidents too, but on the whole it is astonishing how little resistance these well-armed people put up. Since to-day on the Coast, with all their comforts and improvements, Europeans are

85

only too apt to grumble and complain, the way those early pioneers took daily hardships and danger for granted is remarkable ; they not only did not grumble, they uncomplainingly died. There is a tombstone in Freetown to a poor young man who survived but three weeks in this "pestilential climate."

In 1900 the Royal Niger Company's Charter was revoked, since it was felt that a normal government should be set up. Colonel (later Lord) Lugard became the first High Commissioner of Northern Nigeria, and his primary task was to get the place cleaned up. The Royal Niger Company had little influence away from the rivers, though some of their servants had travelled inland and had seen many of the important chiefs. Slave-raiding was the great popular sport still, and it had to be stopped.

By 1902 the country was occupied as far as Zaria. In 1903 Maloney, the Resident at Keffi, was killed by the representative there of the Emir of Zaria, the murderer fleeing to Kano. A hastily formed column marched after him, but Kano refused to give him up ; a single shell, however, into one of the gates of that famous walled city caused the murderer to flee to Sokoto, the Emir of Kano with him. Next morning Kano was running smoothly under the Emir's remaining officials, all except the slave market and the prison. The former was closed ; the latter was opened, to reveal such a scene of horror as showed what high time it was, in the name of suffering humanity, that a strong government should take control. Even now the report, calm and factual, makes sickening reading.

The column hurried on to Sokoto, taking dreadful risks, across the waterless bush, and after a brief skirmish the Fulani Emirs surrendered. Lord Lugard reinstated most of them, but appointed British Residents as advisers. It was a daring gamble, but it worked ; and so like another Cortes, only a shrewder and kindlier one, the little man with a heavy moustache added at a stroke 200,000 square miles to the Empire. That is one way of looking at it, but it is also true to say that he saved over ten million people from slavery, misrule, and despair.

It was a good day's work, but it was not finished. The country had still to be organized, services to be set up, and the desert made to flower like a garden. Steadily Lugard set to work, and travelled and talked and wrote and planned and arranged. In those days it must all have seemed a hopeless task, since there was neither staff nor money nor anyone with experience of administration nor sufficient technical officers —and yet the thing had genuine life in it, and behold it has lived. It is not in perfect working order yet, but things are steadily improving.

After that there was scarcely any trouble. Troops were used on a few occasions, but never in such strength as the great " army " of over a thousand men with which Lugard overthrew so many kingdoms.

The impression must not be gathered from all this that the native peoples of Nigeria are cruel and brutal, since that would be grossly inaccurate and unjust. It was a few unprincipled rulers suffering from too much absolute power who were cruel. The ordinary men and women of Nigeria are kindly and sympathetic folk, who, when they realize that something is wrong, are always ready to do what they can to help. They may not always go about things in what we would think the right way ; but then not all people think alike. It is a striking thing that native courts, far from being harsh, are usually too lenient in their sentences. These industrious, patient people are only nowadays beginning to get their chance to show what they are made of.

Until 1914 Northern and Southern Nigeria ran as two separate administrations, but it was obvious that they were mutually dependent and must one day be combined. In 1912 Lugard was appointed Governor of each individually, to become Governor-General of all Nigeria on 1st January 1914, the year of the outbreak of the first Great War, a most unfortunate date for the amalgamation, since the great task required time and leisure. Within seven months Nigerian troops were fighting the Germans in Kamerun, and later a brigade went to East Africa. The young colony wanted all the staff it could get ; it got scarcely any new staff for five years. It wanted a growing world trade to cover its development ; it came into being with a world of strangled transport and of effort concentrated on the war. Even after the war supplies and transport were difficult to procure, so that progress was still slowed down.

In the years between the wars a great deal has been done, especially in agriculture and forestry, but a great deal remains still to do. Better water supplies, medical services, and education are urgently wanted. So far the country has had little chance, but its chance will, we hope, come before very long.

Chapter VI

BELIEFS AND SUPERSTITIONS

Islam

IN Nigeria there are Moslems, Christians, and Animists. If one asks the ordinary European what he knows about Islam he will almost certainly first mention polygamy, with a background of the *Arabian Nights*. In fact, however, very few Moslems can afford more than one wife. It is true that the law allows wives to be changed, but divorce is not very much more common than elsewhere. In practice there is the same tendency for married couples to keep together as there is elsewhere in the world. But the system of early betrothal and marriage so common in Nigeria makes easy divorce a necessity.

Moslem Law runs all over the Moslem north of Nigeria. The Quran lays down rules for almost every detail of the Moslem's daily life and gives him a social code of some value. In many respects it is a comprehensive code, and a great number of the changes and chances of modern life fall as easily into its embrace as did those of the old days. But of course, since it is thought divinely inspired, it cannot be amended. It is administered in the Native Courts by the Native judges, many of whom are very learned in its intricacies. To listen to an argument between two of them in Hausa on a fine point of legal interpretation is an unforgetable experience. There was an old Alkali, or judge, of Bauchi who was so great an authority that Courts all over the north appealed to him unofficially for guidance on Moslem Law. It was a privilege to listen to him, for he had a very lucid mind and a charming manner and nature.

The Moslem Courts do not allow British-trained barristers, natives though they are, to appear before them. It would be absurd to have pleadings by people who have little or no specialized knowledge of Moslem Law and less of the native customs that may be involved ; for, strange as it may seem, the trained African mind is much further from the bush native than is the European, and has a contempt for him that the European never has. The result is, of course, that the British-trained African barristers try to discredit these Courts ; but in fact though the courts are certainly not perfect, they are effective enough.

There are mosques all over the Islamic areas, and in the great Yoruba cities and in Lagos. Few of these are important structures and almost all are of mud. Most of them are small buildings, but some are larger : in internal appearance, a maze of thick pillars with a low roof. There are no minarets ; the muezzins call to prayer from a short mud stairway set against the mosque wall. In Katsina there is a fine new mosque in concrete, and a new one is being built in Kano. Yet the commonest Moslem meeting-place is not a building at all, but a little " prayer space " marked off with logs of wood or a fence, making a rectangle with an alcove for the " leader " at the east end. These prayer spaces are to be found in every Moslem village.

Christianity

In Nigeria there is and has been for many years a strong Christian Church ; indeed the first Europeans in Abeokuta, just a hundred years ago, were missionaries. All over the south are mission churches and schools, and their civilizing influence has been immense.[1] But in the north Christian

[1] There are about a million Christians of all denominations in Nigeria.

Enugu : Muslim recruits to the R.W.A.F.F. at prayers, led by the
official Imam, who holds the rank of honorary sergeant-major

Kano : house of a rich merchant.   The mud ornamentation of the façade incorporates traditional motifs

A follower of the Shehu of Bornu : his horse is gay with coloured trappings and silver-plated headgear

activities have hitherto been restricted, since Lord Lugard promised the chiefs that there should be no interference with the tribes' own religions. Moreover, in the minds of the ignorant, preaching and teaching by Europeans and their associates would automatically assume the sanction of the Government.

Unhappily there are different sects of Christianity, and sectarianism makes life extremely complicated for the would-be convert. It is a pity that sectarian rivalries still persist in what is virtually the front line. Conversion might well have been restricted to the greater denominations; and the ideal would be for a single Christianity to have been presented by the missionary effort.

One station I was in particularly illustrated the difficulty. It was a primitive place and sparsely populated, yet the way the different missions succeeded one another in influence was astonishing. I had one mason-bricklayer who in a short time managed to change his belief numerous times; an aspen character no doubt, a man of straw blown by every wind, but not untypical. After being pagan and then Moslem, he became in turn Church of England, Roman Catholic, Seventh Day Adventist, and Wesleyan. Any such change is taken very seriously. On my cook's coming back from the town one day with an unusually virtuous expression, I asked him anxiously what was the matter. He said he had been building a church. I said, " That must be the new Roman Catholic one." But since he was at that time an ardent Anglican, he was horrified at the suggestion.

In the same place occurred what might easily have become a dangerous difference between Anglicans and Roman Catholics. Neither body had any European ministers and both were new and looking for converts. Dancing in the streets was very popular there, the young men collecting

7

round a drummer and a piper and slowly shuffling through the dust, making their movements with earnestness and decorum. Now it was a rule of the town that if two parties should meet while dancing, the smaller one should at once give way to the larger; and it so happened that one Christmas Eve a large-sized Protestant dancing party met a Catholic one, which, being numerically much smaller, ought to have given way, but in point of fact decided to stand its ground. So both parties went on dancing in their respective situations far into the night. The same *contretemps* happened on a second occasion, and then a third—this time on New Year's Night, a most important celebration. Flesh and blood could stand it no longer, and the two parties finding mutual recrimination insufficient thereupon fell to blows—I could hear the noise of the fracas from my house a good mile away. Soon the chief's son came up on his bicycle and almost breathless cried, "Father tells me to come to you to say the Christians are killing one another." So I hastened down on my motor bicycle to the scene, to find myself in the centre of a seething, screaming mob. The only check on it came from the old men of the community, who were solemnly running round prodding people in the stomach and crying, "Now do be good and put down that stick." Of course no one took the slightest notice of them, and the parties went on grimly fighting—though few got much injured. Seeing how things stood I mobilized the Native Administration police round me, and soon we had the combatants quelled and sitting on the ground in two muttering groups. The "unhappy heathen," on the other hand, were sitting round on the rocks splitting their sides with laughter at this war in heaven. We proceeded to pile up the sticks and weapons of the combatants and then to burn them, while I preached the people a much-needed sermon freely interlarded with texts. It was either that sermon or the interdiction I put on dancing at night till further notice that made them all creep away very thoughtfully to their homes. As the order affected the pagans as well as the Christians, the latter were correspondingly unpopular. The town was quiet for months afterwards.

The larger towns in the south have many churches, of every shade of opinion, which are crammed with people on a Sunday and loud with the singing of innumerable hymns. Most of the bigger churches have some form of school attached to them. Some of these schools, for both boys and girls, are very good and have white staffs; others are unsatisfactory. There is not enough inspection, supervision, and control to keep up a standard, and the teachers are too often of inferior quality. The mission's best field is medical, and here they have done invaluable work. A recent fine effort is a great attack on leprosy opened by the church militant.

In Lagos there are three cathedrals. The Roman Catholic Cathedral was built before the war, but that of the Church of England, though begun in April 1925, was only completed in 1946; it stands on the water's edge. The Catholic cathedral has great dignity, with its slender concrete flying buttresses; and a simple illuminated cross on the western gable can be seen by night far out at sea. The Church of England structure is a lofty one, built to the plans of a local African architect. The third cathedral is called Bethel: it is very large, but otherwise undistinguished. All three cathedrals are built in local brick plastered over.

There are two Anglican dioceses, those of Lagos and the Niger, and two Roman Catholic bishoprics. The Anglican bishops are Europeans, but among their assistants are three African bishops. The newest is thought to be the first African consecrated on African soil, though there may have been others in the early days of the Church in the Mediterranean.

Much has been written about missionary work, and I do not propose to add to it. I should like, however, to pay my tribute to their labours, often unrecognized and always ill-paid.

One of the most restful places in Lagos is the Colonial Church, a small concrete building which is simple and pleasing. It stands by the racecourse behind Government House in a lovely green compound, and round its porches stand tubs of brilliant flowers. It has a good organ and an enterprising choir. Lagos is proud of it as a local effort, since the congregation built the church and furnished it, and pays for the chaplain and all other expenses. It is primarily a church for the white people in Lagos, by whom it is supported, but Africans in small numbers have often attended and are welcome.

Animism

Animism is not easy to classify since many shades of heathenism are included under the name. There is more than a tendency to make the word mean " everyone else " after one has said Moslem and Christian. The ancient Greeks were animists in their worship of spirits inhabiting the rocks and trees, but not in their conception of the Olympian gods. However, possibly the theory might be stretched to cover even these, since the strangely assorted figures living on that great peak personified human interests and desires. But strictly speaking, an animist is a person who believes in and fears spirits, especially those dwelling in natural objects, and seeks to propitiate them. Practically all the Africans in Nigeria, except a few very devout Moslems and Christians, are in fact animists, hotly though they would deny this. Animism is inherent in their lives, and though they may profess and sincerely believe in their own formally accepted creed, their traditional feeling for these spirits still persists.

As you walk through the bush you may find a little screen of palm fronds, apparently enclosing nothing, and below the screen a pot of palm oil or a decomposing piece of chicken ; but of course you are wrong when you say there is nothing there. You may find, in the heart of a grove, a little grubby house festooned with dirty bits of cloth, hung with old bones and the heads of long-dead animals. This is a place where Africans, otherwise brave and upright, fear to walk or talk freely. The little shrine may be inside a compound wall and there may be an old man there who, rather vaguely, looks after things. Round the hut there may be images, perhaps brightly coloured, which sophisticated Europe regards as high art, but which are too often only the product of incompetent workmanship and wrong thinking. But that is not the point. Behind the screen, near that pot, inside that house, inside the compound, there is just nothing. There cannot be anything there when only spirits are worshipped. The images themselves are not worshipped ; they are merely the messengers and servants of the spirits. Just as an earthly chief has people lolling on his veranda idly thinking of this and that, so the spirits must have these little wooden things, with their ample signs of virility, ready to do their bidding.

The spirits may be appeased by the sacrifice of a chicken or by a libation of palm oil or a mug of beer ; or on important occasions a goat will be killed. No day can be started, no work undertaken, no journey begun, no house planned, no farm cleared, before the appropriate spirits have been appeased by sacrifice or libation. That is why chickens are dearer in the south than they are in the Moslem areas.

The spirits must be consulted on many accounts, and their guidance sought, and that is where the juju-man, or witch-doctor, chiefly comes in. He has many methods of consulting them, a typical divination being carried out by throwing a handful of kola nuts or certain kinds of beans or what not. On the manner in which these fall, some the right way up and others upside down, and on the patterns they make, depends the answer to the question asked.

Sometimes the jujus have been built up into institutions of more than local importance, as, for example, in the last century the Long Juju of Aro Chuku near Calabar, with a sacred cave as the centre at once of a profitable cult and a particularly ruthless trade in slaves. There was a stiff fight before the oracle was dispersed, imprisoned slaves were freed, and the cave was blown in.

As with European witchcraft, the jujus or spells can exert an evil influence physically, since the ordinary African is very susceptible to suggestion properly disguised ; and not seldom have people been known actually to die through the spells put on them. But jujus are not necessarily harmful. There is, for example, the one that protects farm produce left by the roadside. Walking along a path through the bush in Nigeria one may notice every here and there a stack of merchandize unattended—perhaps a pile of yams or a heap of millet or a bundle of firewood. The pile is tied with a grass rope, and at the top a peculiar knot is seen with an end of rope sticking out rather oddly. This means that the produce has been committed to the spirit of the farms for safe custody : anyone, except the owner, who touches it does so at his own risk, and if he should take it away without permission, severe punishment will overtake him, say his hand or foot will fall off. That is a very strong juju indeed. The crops are, after all, the most important thing there is, and I have even seen the juju used in strictly Moslem areas. Produce so protected is never touched except by its owner.

Here is another example of a beneficial juju. My wife and I were staying in a rest-house when one evening the place was threatened by a vast column of driver ants, the most terrible of all pests in Nigeria. We tried all the usual ways of halting the ants, but they came on inexorably. Then I sent for the leading juju-man, a ragged old fellow, very frail of body. He came and looked at the ants. Then with an ordinary knife he cut a thin line right round the house, muttering to himself as he did so. No ants crossed that line, though their direct way obviously would have been across it.

At certain seasons of the year there are dances of the jujus. The women keep indoors, and the men, wearing fantastic masks, prance about the village. Such ceremonies are sometimes used for the anonymous punishment of those who have in some way offended against village opinion. They are an eerie thing to watch: the expressionless faces and the queer music perhaps contribute most to the weird effect, but certainly the most cynical European can hardly see them without a certain qualm.

Charms

The jujus are often a lucky thing for the thief. To steal non-farm produce is no offence, since it is the just punishment of carelessness on the part of the occupier of the house, who should protect himself better. In certain parts of Nigeria when a genuine thief is caught the first thing the police do is to go strictly through his clothes to take from them any odds and ends they can find. Then they take the prisoner away to the cells knowing that all will be well. Were they to overlook any of these things he would probably get through the bars and walk over the sleeping guard to safety! European police officers new to the country laugh at the notion and are rude to their men about it. But the men firmly believe it.

For these odds and ends are regarded as the agencies of spells. Thus there is a powder a little of which blown into the house will put all the inmates to sleep ; there is a small piece of cotton lint which, held in the hand, will make the holder invisible ; and other things make the thief bullet-proof, or impossible to be got hold of, or able to burst open the strongest handcuffs. According to the police the handcuff one is particularly effective, and I have known authentic cases of men who left unopened handcuffs behind them.

I was once badly deceived by a powder juju. It was my first case in the old Provincial Court. For some reason the Native Court could not take it, and I heard the evidence. Part of this was that the thief had been seen creeping about the room at night with a *light in his hand*—two or three people in the room had seen the light. The thief pleaded that there was a conspiracy against him and that he was really a lodger there and had not broken in. The fact that the prosecution had proved he had carried a light was sufficient for me and I acquitted the accused. But I was wrong. To the native mind that was the essential proof of his guilt. He must have used the sleeping powder, and so had felt quite at liberty to walk about the house with a light. The fact that he had been seen merely showed that the powder having lost its value, the inmates had unexpectedly remained awake ! I was the sole person with doubt at all that he was the thief. So his luck was in after all !

Rain-making

One of the most interesting of the magic-workers is the rain-maker, with whom from time to time I have had a good deal to do. He is mostly found in hilly country. In Kabba there even seemed to be a rain-maker in every group of hills, and if a village had once been on the hills and had come down into the plains, as many of them had, there was still a rain-maker in that village.

The rain-maker claims power to control the rain. In a country of intermittent rainfall he is very important, especially as too much rain or rain at the wrong time can do as much harm as too little. In theory he is supposed to be able to bring rain when he wants it, and the method he employs is that of " sympathetic " magic, which means that he pours out water, gruel, blood, or whatever it may be, on the ground after, before, or during certain ceremonies, and the pouring of this fluid forms a symbol of the fall of rain. He may also wear black clothes or have black feathers in his headgear to symbolize the dark rain-clouds.

Evidence is hard to collect on the efficacy of rain-making. Of course the local population believes in it thoroughly, and so do many other people, nor is this surprising in view of much success. Since too much rain is as important as too little, the rain-maker must also be a rain-stopper. When I was running the Kabba and the Okeni divisions together in 1924 I made friends with the head rain-maker of the Igbirras, who was a delightful old man. We had a number of very difficult bridges on the Okeni-Lokoja road (to-day rebuilt), and he was very obliging in letting it rain on the ground below the road only, when the Resident drove along it.

One day he came up to see me and I told him that I was leaving the next morning for Kabba, twenty-five miles by road, but I hoped to be met by a lorry somewhere on the Kabba side. The boundary between the two territories was about half-way. It was at the very height of the Rains, in August. The old man looked a bit depressed and said it was a bad time of year for him to help me and everything was against it. He thought for a while and then said that as far as the boundary it would probably be all right. After that he had no authority. Next morning I set out, and it was as grim a day as I have ever seen. There was a horrible chill about the air, which goes with rain, and great black clouds hung over the tops of the granite hills about the road; swathes of mist, the lower edges of the clouds, trailed in the little valleys. For twelve miles I walked through this kind of weather, which grew worse and worse, but it did not actually rain until I had crossed the boundary. A short distance on the other side the rain came down in sheets.

A couple of years later my wife and I arrived at a rest-house about eighteen miles north of Kabba. From our point of view the village headman was ineffective, and when I saw that a large hole was still to be seen in the grass roof of the rest-house, as it had been four or five months before, I was not very pleased—and said so. This again was at the height of the Rains, and as we were making bridges on the new Kabba-Isanlu road, we were going to be there for a week or so. He asked, "What are you worried about anyhow?" and I said, "Well, naturally, we are going to be here for a bit and we don't want to get wet, as we certainly will with that great hole in the roof." And then he answered, "If you get wet while you're here in this house you can do what you like with me; but I don't think you will." For over a week we lived there. There were black clouds everywhere, and it rained heavily in the village a few hundred yards away, even spotted once or twice with us, but during that time it never once rained on the rest-house itself. Of course it is just coincidence; it *must* be or the foundations of the earth are insecure, but it is a strange coincidence all the same, the like of which I have frequently experienced.

But I experienced cases of failure too. When we were making the Kabba-Lokoja road in the heart of the rain-maker's country we had to do a lot of "cut and fill" work, and the ground was so hard that our steel picks began to get worn down; indeed in the end they were only about five inches long. A good fall of rain would have been a godsend. At length I sent for the best known rain-maker in the area and offered him £5 if he could produce rain in a certain number of days. £5 was a lot of money in those days, and he worked very hard for it, but he failed. No doubt there were the usual technical excuses, and, in fact, everything was against him—the weather was set fair, the sky was as hard as bronze, and the wind was wrong. But the excuses he actually offered were unconvincing and irrelevant.

It is a change to go from the rain-makers' country to that of the Moslem Hausa, where no-one will ever admit anything about the probabilities of rain. If you say to a Moslem, " Is it going to rain this morning ? " he will answer, " It is in the hands of God." That is sound doctrine, but it does not tell you whether you should take a raincoat with you or not.

Chapter Seven

NIGERIA ADVANCES

THE conception of " development," in practice as in theory, conjures up different pictures in different people's minds. This is no less true of Nigeria than elsewhere, and there are many people there who have pet remedies and panaceas, who cling to a single word that will solve all troubles, or to a phrase that will dissolve all difficulties, despite the obvious fact that both causes and cures are obscure and complex matters. Just as people in Britain cry " Free trade " or " Nationalize the banks," and think that all problems are thereby removed, so in the matter of colonial development people think that words like " education " or " village industries " are the complete answer to all questions. Then others think the answer lies in factories and miles of terraces and trams, others in the spread and development of " culture " of various kinds, and still others in the hunt for new markets. Yet all of them are right to some extent and true development must take cognizance of all of them together—there must be political progress, industrial and commercial advance, and cultural development, and they must be integrated. That is what makes the problem difficult, especially in a community so generally backward as that of Nigeria. There is so much to do and so little that can be left undone without serious loss. All the different interests must have their heads as far as possible and yet none must get out of hand : health and education, land cultivation and local industries, administration and government, are indissolubly bound together. Trade goes with them, though not much can be done about that without good communications and housing. Education is essential, since there are large numbers of jobs that will have to be filled by trained men ; health is essential, since those who are suffering from malnutrition or intestinal parasites cannot get the best out of education ; and money is essential. Moreover, the schemes for the future must be of general application and yet they must be capable of elastic adjustment in detail for varied circumstances.

The time for piecemeal advances has gone by and the world is watching to see what Britain is going to make of this vast heritage. Some of the work can be done with existing means and funds, but for real advance the problem is where the requisite additional money is to come from. When the development schemes have had time to ripen there will be money accruing from them, but that will not be for many years, and the interim is the difficulty.

But what has been done so far ? Undoubtedly a good deal, but not just to make the officials' life comfortable ; indeed the officials' life has not been made as comfortable as it might be. I well remember the mixed scorn and astonishment in an American airman's voice when, talking about the lack of piped water in a small Government station, he said, " And did you say you British had been in this country *forty* years ? " It was difficult to answer quickly and convincingly, since the questioner was not likely to understand that what is rather condescendingly called " creature comforts " had to be neglected when there were other things to be done ; yet in fact to some extent he was right, for that particular station was one where comfort was vital to efficient work. But it was impossible to describe concisely what original conditions we had found and what we had done to improve them.

Development was possible on a large scale only after the first World War. Before that time the country was still being opened up, and administration, even in the south, was in its infancy. There were few roads and bridges, the eastern railway line was still building and the northern extensions were only at the blueprint stage. Staff was new and quite inexperienced, and many departments had poor organization at headquarters. We were only in the experimental stage until well after 1918 and did not rightly know what we were aiming at. But since then there has been a change, despite the set-back of the 1929–30 slump—and the slump was serious. A slump means immediate curtailment of revenue, and that in its turn means reduction of expenditure which is inevitably unequal in incidence. All departments have a certain number of items in their budgets that can be eliminated without reducing efficiency, but when they have been cut the tendency is to look round for further items to axe, and the newest developments are as a rule the ones chosen. Thus in the medical field, hospitals must be maintained at all costs, with their staffs and equipment, but new sanitary schemes, drainage works, research undertakings, not being indispensable, are things that can be sacrificed. A period of slump and " cuts " is thus a foe to development. Our slump was bad: we lost revenue, we had cuts in salary, we stopped recruiting new staff, and we economized in every conceivable way. In fact it was a nauseating period, when there seemed an evil spirit abroad, the ill effects arising from which still persist. The depression took a long time to dissipate, and it took years to make up the lost way—indeed we had just made it up before the war of 1939–45 started. If someone would give us twenty years of peace and financial stability we could change the face of Nigeria.

Material Progress

In spite of the slump and other obstacles that followed the first World War, a good deal has been done. In 1921 there was only the direct line of railway to Kano with a light branch to Jos and a stretch of 150 miles from Port Harcourt to Enugu ; since then the eastern line has been joined with the main line at Kaduna and a branch has gone to Jos ; two more branches of the western line have been built, each about 140 miles long, and a great deal of the old main line has been relaid with heavier metal. Bridges have been replaced and stations and junctions replanned and rebuilt.

Similarly, roads have been built in every Province and many of our old rough efforts have been remodelled and rebridged. In 1921 there were 2,000 miles of motorable road : there are over 20,000 now, and we want another 20,000 again.

The harbour at Lagos was constructed to its first stage, that at Port Harcourt completed. Roads were tarred in the towns ; new designs of houses and offices were planned and carried out ; electric light schemes and waterworks were built in the larger centres (though there is still much to do) ; complete new government stations were erected, and along the new roads trading stations were built. To-day good prices can be got by local farmers at places that a few years ago would have been thought to be far in the bush ; and tin and gold miners can prospect and mine to their hearts' content in perfect safety where not long ago men went about armed. Major airfields have been cleared, runways made in eight places, and over twenty smaller fields prepared. The big problem of trunk telephones is being tackled, and most places of any size have telephone exchanges. One can telephone to-day over most of the Western and Eastern

Provinces, and over at least the centre of the Northern Provinces.

The Forestry Department have made reserves of standing timber in all Provinces and have been trying to combat the menace of erosion.

Agricultural officials have been experimenting with farms of all types. The veterinary officials have brought under control the more serious diseases which threatened the lives of herds of fine cattle ; their supervision of the industry in hides (cattle) and skins (goats and sheep)—which now promises a great future—is beginning to produce results.

Cathedrals, churches, chapels, colleges, and mosques have been erected all over the country. Education has begun to spread and girls' education, even in the exclusively Moslem areas, has taken very successful root. The Yaba College outside Lagos is turning out a number of young engineers and doctors of a fair standard.

In almost every big town there is now an African hospital where the government maintains a medical officer and a nursing sister. But as the countryside was scarcely touched at all, about 1930 the provision of dispensaries was started, and a good many were built by the Native Administrations to standard patterns with trained attendants at each. Unfortunately since then these dispensaries have fallen on evil days, for it has been found impossible to provide enough medical officers to have them adequately inspected and kept efficient.

Political organization too has gone ahead and there have been marked advances in the efficiency of the Native Administrations in respect of their treasuries, the training of their police, the organization of their prisons, their court work, and the training and conditions of service of their greatly enlarged African staffs. The Government departments too have made big strides forward.

The Nigeria Regiment: bandsmen in full-dress uniform

Miners going to work at the Government Colliery, Enugu, which produces ample coal for Nigeria's domestic use

Mud houses of the so-called " pagans " of the Nigerian Plateau

The new town of Takalafiya.   A sleeping sickness experiment :
the huts are spaced twelve feet apart in the compound

The all-over progress, then, has been good, and we are not ashamed of our efforts—we should be fools and hypocrites if we were. But we could have done more had more money been available. For all these things have been done without any aid from the United Kingdom Treasury. People in Britain are apt to think that a Nigerian official receives his salary from the Home Treasury, and are astonished to hear that all Nigerian salaries are paid for by Nigeria from Nigerian revenue raised in Nigeria.

This revenue amounts to about £14,000,000 (twelve shillings per head), the chief items in which come from customs charges and from direct taxation of Europeans and Africans. As for expenditure, no small part goes to the salaries of civil servants, the provision of pensions, and such general items as stores and supplies, transport, new constructions, and emergency outlays. But until quite recently the Colonial Office maintained the principle that a Colony must be completely self-supporting ; which was unquestionably sound, since it fortified self-respect and a sense of responsibility, and formed a strong inducement to put forth the best possible efforts.

But changed world conditions now render the strict observance of the rule inexpedient, and Britain, realizing that she must take steps to implement her promise to help the Colonial peoples, has instituted a Colonial Development Fund. For it is obvious that a huge country with a population of low earning-power cannot itself finance the gigantic development schemes required to bring it up to the standards of to-day. Moreover even normal public services are much more costly than formerly, partly through a world rise in prices, and partly because up-to-date equipment is expensive and required in great quantities—thus X-ray apparatus, once a luxury of medical provision, now plays an essential part in routine practice.

Native Education

The educated African is apt to think of little but obtaining the right of self-government, and to forget the vital need for self-help in matters of health, sanitation, and improved land cultivation. He presses for higher education, but largely because the possession of certain diplomas and degrees is the qualification for secure, black-coated jobs. There is a certain groping for culture, but too often of a mistaken kind and for mistaken reasons. A recent Lagos newspaper article pleaded for the education of girls to be extended, on the ground that it would be pleasant to have a wife with whom one could "discuss Shakespeare, Addison, and Southey"! Certainly a wider measure of native education is an urgent need, but the first step is the most difficult—to decide what that education ought to be, in terms of aim, curriculum, and methods. The present educational system, since it is largely planned to suit an arid European examination syllabus, is too far removed from practice and the assimilation of the best in Nigerian native culture. But what to replace it by is another matter. Health training ought undoubtedly to play a prominent part in it, the home background and tradition should be studied before European history and geography are taken, there should be abundant practical work, and there should be practical and visual approaches made to the chief matters studied, which should be motivated to promote a sense of citizenship and responsibility.

But the formulation of good schemes is not enough: teacher-training too is required. One of the weaknesses of the existing system is the poor standard of too many of the teachers, who read little themselves unless it be the newspapers, and tend to teach parrot-fashion subjects they know by heart but do not fully understand. Such teachers can recite principles faultlessly, but have no conception of how to apply them. The teacher's difficulties are added to by the fact that there is rarely any home background of reading or knowledge to help make school work real. There are very few educated African women, and of these only a small proportion persevere with their education after marriage. The child is thus unsupported culturally at school, and in his home he has no books at all, except any textbooks he takes there himself. There is no children's magazine or boys' or girls' paper for him to read ; and when he leaves school he soon loses his small and uncertain learning through the absolute book famine in the land. The few books that are on the market are often unsuitable for one reason or another, and they are far too expensive to buy. A book at three shillings, which is not expensive by our standards, means as a rule a day's pay ; and that is a prohibitive price for anyone. Part of the solution is the provision of libraries, particularly for the more expensive books, but there can be no satisfactory solution that does not include the supply of books cheap enough for children and adults to buy for themselves. The demand exists.

During the war we set up reading-rooms in the larger centres, and about 185 were in use. They issued war news and information about the war. Since then the focus has shifted to general reading. While there are periodicals and newspapers, it has proved nearly impossible to obtain books, either new or second-hand. This is a pity, as the reading-rooms are popular and well attended. Some are centres for literary societies which arrange lectures and debates.

Self-government

The vast mass of the people are not interested at all in the demand for self-government, which comes from a small but vocal educated minority. Even when the conception is explained patiently to them it makes little appeal, since they well know that they already enjoy ample freedom of action in the management of their own affairs, and that government under the sole control of the wealthy and educated Africans of the cities might be an exchange for the worse.

The pity of it is that the educated Africans seem entirely to fail to realize that they have the true seed of self-government in their Native Administrations. Few take much interest in these bodies, and it is noticeable that where most educated Nigerians come from—the Eastern Provinces—is precisely where there are the fewest flourishing Native Administrations. The practice and tradition of local self-government in Britain enriched the country's political experience and fitted it to develop the institutions of democratic central government. So it might be in Nigeria, if the educated and influential Africans would actively participate everywhere in their own local government.

The wish for self-government is natural and reasonable enough when it confines itself to a demand for it within the framework of the Empire, acknowledging the advantages that have undoubtedly derived from the Empire association and the continuing need for British guidance for a long time to come. But on the part of some extremists these last conditions are not observed. However, Britain is committed to the ultimate grant of self-government to Nigeria, and the aim of the existing administration is to help the country on its way to fitness for that step—for in any circumstances political consciousness is very slow indeed in developing. But little advance will be possible, political or otherwise, until health standards are higher ; disease is the scourge of Nigeria.

The Struggle Against Disease

The record of health of the Africans in Nigeria is unhappily a very bad one. Although they are immune to many deadly diseases afflicting the European, they are particularly prone to succumb to others ; and except in a few localities the great battle against malaria, yellow fever, sleeping sickness, and leprosy has scarcely begun. The magnitude of the problem is appalling. It is so even in immediate necessities, as one will realize when estimating the amount of quinine alone necessary for the adequate treatment of over twenty million people, or the amount of labour demanded by drainage schemes for eliminating the mosquito from a huge area like Nigeria. On the other hand the difficulties could be much reduced if self-help were widely adopted. Thus if every town and village were to make a serious attempt, with skilled supervision, to drain its own neighbourhood, within ten years malaria's incidence would be markedly reduced ; or if it strove to cope with its own elementary sanitary problems, again with skilled supervision, dysentery would definitely receive a setback.

Venereal disease and yaws could be to a large extent combated, but organized propaganda is required to induce sufferers to go to the clinics and dispensaries. Leprosy and tuberculosis demand lengthy treatment, but at least the first steps could be taken by the villagers themselves ; witness how in Europe leprosy was stamped out as a result of local segregation on local initiative and without the use of modern medicines and drugs. Sleeping sickness can be dealt with, but costs are high, since to produce lasting effects whole areas would have to be cleared and replanned. So far there is one settlement where good work has been done, but this is only a small beginning. Cerebro-spinal meningitis claims its victims by tens of thousands at a time, and countless people suffer from dysentery and the other water-borne diseases—hookworm in the intestines, guinea worm in the legs, bilharzia in the kidneys, and others throughout the body.

Then, too, lunacy and blindness are widely prevalent. The first is costly to deal with, as both buildings and special staff are required ; the second is less costly, but demands as much trained and sympathetic care. As for their incidence, the number of mental cases in Nigeria has not been estimated, though it is known to be high, and the blind are to be seen everywhere.

Such is the long and appalling record of serious disease, without making any mention of the innumerable ordinary ailments requiring attention day by day. Clinics, dispensaries, hospitals, and all the staff, both black and white, needed to run them are an insistent and never-ceasing demand ; but the magnitude of the task is overwhelming and supply must take a very long time to catch up with it. A little has already been done ; experience has been gained, and the confidence won of hundreds of thousands, who will be the means in years to come of securing that of the millions remaining. But until health conditions and controls are immeasurably advanced beyond the present standards, it is obvious that little that is effective can be done about matters of wider moment to the country's development and well-being.

Present Projects

Under the stimulus of the Colonial Development and Welfare Act, from which Nigeria has been promised £23,000,000 over ten years, all departments have prepared general plans for development and are now working on details. The intention is that many of them should be revenue-producing, for Nigeria must rely on its own resources and not on world demand. There was an example of this danger in the inter-war period, when the palm oil trade went from prosperity to depression and back again in a series of hysterical waves. The best policy would seem to be the building up of a strong internal trade in foodstuffs, which will help among other things to correct dietetic deficiencies, a very serious matter in Nigeria.

One of the lines of development cheapest to pursue, yet likely to return better dividends than almost any other, is co-operation. A few years before the war experiments were started with this end in view, and good progress was made. Co-operation demands a good educational standard if it is to run smoothly, but otherwise it is not difficult. There is a great future for it. If co-operation can be got going all over the country, many of the present trading difficulties will pass and it will be possible to build up a considerable internal trade which may be counted on to yield long-term prosperity. Once twenty million people start working together with mutual confidence anything is possible. Co-operation is probably the only system capable of producing such confidence ; at least so far it has proved the only innovation to create a body of public opinion of its own. Moreover, with a strong body of public opinion behind it, we shall see the end of a good deal of the bribery and corruption that impair the life of Nigeria to-day.

The business houses of Nigeria have post-war planning to face up to, in order to provide the consumer with high quality British goods at reasonable prices. The confidence of the people must be retained by conspicuous fair dealing if the trader and the country are both to be prosperous.

The mines have been rumoured for twenty years to be coming to the end of their yield of tin, yet they are still successfully productive. Other metals are being prospected and worked, among which are gold, mica, columbite, ilmenite, wolfram, and tungsten. A vast area of iron-ore-bearing rock has been located, and the large coalfield in the Eastern Provinces is being opened up by the Government colliery.

The Railway, the Marine, and the Public Works Departments will have to cope with increased demands for transport arising out of post-war conditions. Urgent water supply and irrigation schemes will need expert staffs in the Public Works, Survey, and Geological Survey Departments. The construction of houses, offices, and public buildings to suit the tastes and requirements of officials has been the exacting duty of the Director of Public Works at all times, but in the future the scale of things will be larger and the problem more intricate.

The Veterinary and Agriculture Departments will have to ensure that the people of Nigeria are more efficiently fed, derive advantage from the new crops that the war has shown can be readily produced when the urge is there, and increase the goods for export.

All the Government Departments have an increasing responsibility in view of the prevailing trend towards change and reorganization. A new administrative machine is being steadily built, but the parts will need constant testing and adjusting to eliminate strains and faults. As in the past there will be required a constant exercise of tact to moderate the enthusiasms of the technical departments who are ever after enormous schemes to bring about a new heaven and a new earth, to press on the faint-hearted into action, to encourage the over-anxious (a thankless but perennial task), and to win a measure of public support for whatever developments are projected. For this last purpose Administration has also to determine to-day how the modern forms of publicity, in the hands of the Public Relations Office, can be used to the best advantage ; whether a particular cause is to be promoted by the printing press, photography, cinema film, broadcasting, or loud-speaker van.

With such active days ahead in Nigeria, there is a job for everyone—for the European to give the best possible guidance and leadership, and for the African to acquire skills, to work faithfully for the common good, to suggest improvements, and to lead his brethren. The African needs perhaps most to realize that though the heritage is his, it cannot be allowed to lie fallow, and that in a sense he is Everyman and therefore his brother's keeper.

Chapter Eight

OUTLINES OF ADMINISTRATION

The Governor and His Councils

THE Colonial Empire has evolved, over the last four hundred years, a flexible organization for its governments which has been throughly tried and tested and found on the whole to be sound. The principle observed is that of a twofold sub-division of authority : the sub-division by population and territory (that is, local sub-division), and the sub-division by activities (that is, departmental sub-division).

In local sub-division, detailed control is left to the local administration, working along general lines laid down by the Secretary of State for the Colonies, who is responsible to Parliament. The size of the local areas varies widely, from tiny islands to the great African territories, and their populations are as varied as their sizes, both in magnitude and in stage of political and cultural development. As it were, the general pattern of the suit remains the same, but the cut and the size are modified according to local requirements.

At the head of each administration stands a Governor, appointed by the King, and acting as the King's personal representative. He has many of the Sovereign's powers, including the prerogative of mercy to condemned criminals, and the right of approving local laws (subject to the King's confirmation in due course) and being served first at meals. The conception is easy to grasp and the position of the Governor is more or less the same in all the colonies. But is he an autocrat able to act without taking advice ? The Governor has two official sets of advisers. The first is the small Executive Council, meeting once a week. Certain matters must, by law, be approved by the Governor-in-Council ; others are put to the Executive Council presided over by the Governor, viz. the Chief Secretary, the three Chief Commissioners, the Attorney-General, the Financial Secretary, and the Medical and Education Directors. Others can be nominated, two of the present four being non-official. Most important matters are laid before it, including all legislation before it is published. The Governor may act against its advice, but must give reasons for so doing to the Secretary of State.

The other body is the Legislative Council. This used to be controlled by a majority of official members ; its unofficial members could only criticize and advise. In 1946 a new constitution was enacted on a very different basis. In each of the three Regions, North, East, and West, there is now a House of Assembly of African members selected from the Native Authorities or their Councils, with, in the North, additional members to speak for special interests. The official members are the Residents in charge of the Provinces and the regional heads of the Medical, Agricultural, and Public Works Departments, with a Law Officer. The unofficials have in each a clear majority.

In the North there is also a House of Chiefs. To this come all the First-class Chiefs and ten of the Second-class. They choose four members to go to Legislative Council. From the West two Chiefs are chosen. They are all unofficial members. The unofficial members of each House of Assembly choose from their own number representatives for Legislative Council, where they join three elected members for Lagos and one for Calabar and a few nominated members, making twenty-one in all in addition to six Chiefs.

There are eight *ex-officio* members of Executive Council, plus the Development Secretary, the heads of Agriculture and Public Works, the Commissioners of Labour and of the Colony, and one Resident from each Region. Thus there is an ample unofficial African majority.

Legislative Council and the regional Houses of Assembly debate on parliamentary lines, but so far there is no sign of a party system in the Houses : in the House of Chiefs there is no " Government side." The Regional Houses consider draft legislation and debate a regional budget of revenue and expenditure. They make recommendations to Legislative Council for the acceptance or amendment of bills and financial requirements.

The closest control that Legislative Council has over the country is through the final Estimates (Budget). These Estimates are based on a combination of the regional figures and the amounts required for " central " expenditure : for the preparation and submission of these Estimates the Financial Secretary is responsible. The greater part of the revenue comes from Customs duties and much of the balance from taxation.

Representatives of the Departments attend before the Finance Committees of Legislative Council and of the Regions for cross-examination on their estimates for the ensuing year. The Committees may ask what questions they like and can amend the proposals. When from time to time unforeseen expenditure becomes inevitable, sanction for it has first to be obtained from the appropriate Committee before the Governor's approval can be sought. This again furnishes a valuable detailed control over the government machine.

The Various Departments

The multifarious activities of the Government are divided out among a number of Departments. All Departments have heads, senior officials of great experience but varying in title with their Departments, the commonest titles being Director and Commissioner.

Departments are independent of one another, and usually their staffs are organized into Headquarters and territorial units. In such a huge country as Nigeria there must be some delegation of control of staffs and their activities, and therefore there are territorial sub-divisions with responsible officers in charge of each. Even the smallest territorial sub-division of certain of the Departments—the Posts and Telegraphs, for example—covers an enormous area, and consequently the responsibility of quite subordinate technical officials is considerable. Even a minor contingency like that of leave is a complicated one. In West Africa one quarter of the European staff, apart from people in hospital, is on leave at any given time. The leave allowed is one week for every month of service (and this is richly deserved). When on leave, of course, an officer has to be replaced, and that is quite a problem. This does not apply to sickness, since that is usually not of long duration and a post can be left for a few days without anyone in charge, but should an official fall seriously ill, or become invalided, relief must naturally be given. The posting of reliefs means that organization has to be flexible. There are some people indeed who appear to spend most of their time going round as reliefs ! It is a sore point of the service that certain people get moved round too much ; but as a rule the critics do not realize the grave difficulties to be coped with in distributing staff.

The Chief Secretary

The Governor cannot deal with all these Departments single-handed, and he takes action through his Chief Secretary. This officer is a man of wide experience, usually in other Colonies but not as a rule in Nigeria, and he is the channel by which all matters reach the Governor. The

119

Governor's principal adviser, he is, of course, a member of
Ex. Co., though a great deal of his advice is given on matters
that do not concern that exalted body. Such advice is
tendered by means of the files that are sent up for the
Governor's information or orders. The Chief Secretary is
the head of a Secretariat which is specially staffed by the
Provincial Administrative Service, with a limit of four years'
duty, after which officials must return to their Provinces.
This system ensures that experience is always kept up to
date and that officials do not develop " staff minds."

An official of special importance is the Financial Secretary,
who deals generally with staff—entirely with administrative
staff, and with departmental staff whenever problems of a
general nature arise. He handles all the financial detail of
Government, which, at times, when it comes to balancing
the estimates, is no mean responsibility. A Development
Secretary now deals with the many problems related to
development planning. They share office buildings and
organization with the Chief Secretary, and have administrative officers posted to them from the Provinces in the same
way.

The Courts

The Administration of the Law is somewhat complicated.
There are two kinds of court—the Supreme Court and the
Native Courts—with jurisdiction over largely the same areas.
The Supreme Court is the most important judicial body,
and is presided over by the Chief Justice, whose official
precedence comes immediately after that of the Governor.
This Court has, of course, full rights of trial of criminal and
civil cases of all types over the whole country (its jurisdiction
has changed several times) : wherever it is possible cases are
left to the Native Courts. All members of this court, that is
the judges (who are called unpronounceably " puisne ") and

the magistrates, are professional barristers ; members of the local Bar appear before them, and procedure is just the same as in the United Kingdom.

The Protectorate Court was created in 1933 to replace the much criticized Provincial Courts that were functioning when I went out first. These were criticized because they gave legal power to Residents and District Officers who were not legally qualified. The fact that these officers gave intelligent decisions, were at least intellectually the equal of the barristers, in many cases had a good knowledge of the language spoken by the accused and witnesses, and always had a profound knowledge of their way of life was entirely brushed aside. The Protectorate Court was intended to be manned by professional Judges and Magistrates, though at first most of them were members of the Administrative Service. Its advantage was that Counsel could appear before it. Since it was awkward to have a Supreme Court confined to the Colony (as it was then) and a Protectorate Court over the rest of the country, this was only an interim measure. In 1946 the Protectorate Court was abolished and the jurisdiction of the Supreme Court extended throughout Nigeria. The staff of the one Court was embodied in the other. The District Officer is still *ex officio* a Magistrate and his staff have power to sign warrants. The Judges, some of whom are Africans, have huge areas to cover and spend much of their time on circuit. There are a number of professional Magistrates (some African) in the larger centres.

The Native Courts have been referred to in several places in this book. They now extend over the whole country, except Lagos itself, and have authority over all people whose way of life is purely native. They vary greatly in powers, efficiency, and composition. There are four grades ; the lowest deals only with the simplest cases, the highest, the A grade, of which courts there are few, has powers of life and death. Some courts are composed of a single native judge, some of a bench of leading men, some are so large as to comprise most of the village. Some follow British court procedure rather slavishly, some follow the purest Moslem Law. These courts are closely supervised by the Administrative Staff, and besides there is a regular means of appeal from lowest to highest, and also to the High Court and in some cases the West African Court of Appeal. The Native Courts hear about 115,000 criminal and 240,000 civil cases a year against the Supreme Court's 18,000 criminal trials.

The Groups of Provinces

Nigeria is split into three areas and a bit. The three are called the Northern, Eastern, and Western Provinces, and the bit is the Colony. The Northern Provinces cover about three-quarters of the area of Nigeria, and the Eastern and Western together cover the remaining quarter, the disproportion in size being due to the sparsity of population in the North compared with the other two areas. Administratively the arrangement is a convenient one. The " bit," which is just a strip along the western part of the coastline, is important because it happens to include the Nigerian capital, Lagos.

Each of the Groups of Provinces is controlled by a Chief Commissioner, an important figure in the Government system. He is a member of Ex. Co. and is responsible to the Governor for the administration of his area. He is given an excellent house, a small secretariat, and the style of " His Honour." The Provincial Secretariats, like the Chief Secretary's Office, are staffed from the ordinary run of the Administrative Service. The training they afford is valuable and the constant coming and going of the officers between the bush and the Secretariats has a levelling-down effect—it rubs the rough places off the bush people and blisters the smoothness of the townsmen.

The " Colony " comes under a Commissioner who counts as a Resident, but he is independent of the Chief Commissioners, and directly responsible to the Governor. This is a reasonable arrangement, since the Governor lives in the area. The Colony lies at his door and he can direct things to his own liking without sending orders through a Chief Commissioner living 120 miles off. But the arrangement has the grave defect of over-emphasising what is really only a small fraction of Nigeria. The complex affairs of an international port and of the capital of a country comprising a great diversity of peoples have to be attended to by one official. But he is, of course, assisted by the Departments, and by the Lagos Town Council, of which he is *ex officio* chairman.

In their headquarters towns the Chief Commissioners have at hand representatives of many of the Departments, who can advise them on local matters, and so save continually consulting Lagos. In some towns there are even Heads of Departments, since Heads are not all located in Lagos. Agriculture and Forestry are at Ibadan, the Nigeria Regiment and Geological Survey at Kaduna, the Colliery and Prisons at Enugu, and the Mines at Jos.

The Chief Commissioners' areas are divided into Provinces : twelve in the North, six in the West, and six in the East. Provinces vary a good deal in size and importance. The Plateau Province is 10,423 sq. miles in extent, the Bornu Province 46,000 sq. miles ; Kano has over two and a half million people, Owerri two millions, and Ondo just under half a million. The differences are due to such factors as historical chieftaincies, geographical units, and tribal affinities, but not at all to Administrative convenience. The Province,

9

irrespective of its size, is under a Resident. (There is a small group of officials called Senior Residents, but this is merely a title indicating position in the service, and does not attach to any specific office.)

Provincial Administration

The Northern Resident is as august a being as it is possible to find in the world to-day. This is not the official's fault. Most Northern Residents have been simple retiring men, but the position is thrust upon them and, being men under discipline, they take it. Since few will argue with them, after a while even the most humble are driven to the conclusion that they must always be right—that is, unless a disaster chances. The lucky Resident is one who has with him a senior D.O. who is an old friend, and who is prepared to take a stand when necessary. Then administration is at its best. The Southern Resident is more approachable and lives in less isolated splendour. The occasion of such anomalies between the status of officials is obscure ; perhaps it is " historical momentum " on a small scale.

At his headquarters the Resident has a Provincial Office, and attached to it, in all the Northern and some of the Eastern and Western Provinces, are a young white administrative officer and a number of African clerks. As there is a great deal of paper work to be done, most of the Resident's time is taken up in his office ; and in a busy centre he may have to spend so long on interviews as to need to make up for the lost time by working far into the night. He must also go on tour from time to time to see what is going on in the Divisions.

The Resident must be a man of wide experience. He must be ready to sympathize with the Doctor over staff discipline, to condole with the Engineer on the shortage of metalling, to congratulate the Forestry Officer on the success of his seedlings, to deplore with the Telegraph Engineer the slowness of the clearings under the line, to hold out a friendly hand to the O.C. Troops, who has just got an unkind telegram from his Colonel, and so on and so on. Further, he has to produce solutions to the many knotty problems put to him by these officials and others, and when he goes out on tour for a slight change the D.O. of the place he is visiting is sure to trot out all the problems that *he* has been storing up against the visit. Yet the Resident's life is very tolerable as long as he preserves his sense of humour.

The smallest administrative unit is the Division, of which there are from one to five in a Province. The areas and populations vary from Division to Division, as does the work. Some Divisions are very simple to run, others are nightmares. Some seem to run like clockwork and are never in the news, and others are always in trouble and progress like a bucking horse. The common factor is that they each come under a District Officer. The District Officer may or may not have a junior to help him, but, as a rule, he has far too much to do, having not only to supervise the running of the whole Division, but also to help the Departments to function properly. He must have many and great qualities : the patience of Job, the strength of Hercules, the ubiquity of Mercury, the cunning of Ulysses, the dignity of Menelaus, the wisdom of Nestor, the learning of Athene, the courage of Ajax, and the tongue of Homer himself! All these and more also are the attributes that the appointments staff of the Colonial Office so anxiously search for in their candidates. And they find a good many of them. No one has them all, but all the D.O.s I know, and that runs into hundreds, have some of them. They would be surprised if you told them so, since for the most part they are unassuming fellows, but if they had not these attributes they would fail in their jobs, and that they certainly have not done. A good deal of criticism is heard of the administrative staff, some of it justifiable and some not, but it has never been said that they were incompetent. They live, for the most part, in one-man stations. Some are located on main roads, and they see people passing through ; others are in isolated places where they see only those who purposely visit them. In our first station my wife and I saw only nine white faces in eleven months. We went into Provincial Headquarters from time to time, but few people came to visit us. It was not an easy journey.

Native Administration

It is clearly impossible for the administrative organization I have indicated to reach down to the people themselves. If all the Administrative Officers there are, apart from the Secretariats and those assigned special duties, were allocated equal shares of the population to be responsible for, the number would be about 165,000 persons each. Recourse has therefore to be had to Native Administration. When the British arrived in Nigeria they found the Northern Emirates and the old Yoruba kingdoms organized under chiefs, who by and large were efficient and respected, and had a working pattern of administration, and indeed in certain parts forms of taxation and courts of law. Unless they proved personally unsatisfactory, these chiefs were retained permanently in their positions. The system has since been modified in a number of respects, but government by chiefs to-day is substantially on the tradition first found established. Harsh and unjust practices have been suppressed, properly constituted courts have been set up to administer the kind of law understood in the respective areas, taxation has been regularized, and the chiefs have been given the responsibility of

126

assessing and collecting taxes, and of maintaining peace and good order in their particular areas. For convenience their territory, when above a certain size, has been sub-divided into Districts (under African District Headmen), which again may be sub-divided into Village Areas and Villages (under Village Headmen). The chiefs' success in keeping law and order is the more remarkable in that they command only small local police forces—the brilliantly smart Nigeria Police are not seen outside townships except as escorts for D.O.s on tour—and in the bush only the Village and District Headmen.

Of the taxes they collect, the chiefs retain a share through their Native Treasuries for the payment of salaries and other costs of administration (the chiefs and principal officials receive their salaries from the Native Treasury), covering all phases of activity—courts, police, prisons, schools, hospitals, secretarial and accounts, works, agriculture, forestry, and veterinary. The money for these services has to be estimated for by the chiefs, in a set form, and approved before the financial year opens, as with the central government estimates.

The system of local rule by chiefs may be imperfect, but it works smoothly and satisfactorily enough. The people have every chance to lodge complaints with a white officer, and have little hesitation in doing so, but the number of complaints received, all things considered, is not large, nor is their nature very serious. In certain areas some of the chiefs seem from a British standpoint to be too autocratic, but the tradition is understood and respected. In other areas the tradition itself is democratic. Everywhere development and adaptation have taken place, and most of the chiefs now work amicably with and on the advice of a Council. They have no power to make laws, being subject to the general legislation of the Protectorate, but they are

127

authorized to make rules dealing with local matters of many kinds, as, for instance, housing and markets.

So much for rule by chiefs, but in the creeks, parts of the Plateau, and in the east, there was no immemorial custom of chieftainship, but rather of Village Councils. The problem was to decide what system to adopt there, and the testing place proved to be the Eastern Provinces. Administrative officers too are often cut-and-dried souls who want everything neatly arranged and ticketed as an evident token that the system is working and fool-proof. Since the Northern Provinces worked like clockwork under the rule of the chiefs, these officers assumed that the same system would be best for the other territories, whether they had a chieftainship tradition or not. They therefore initiated the system in the Eastern Provinces, and appointed chiefs everywhere. At first things worked without too much difficulty, but suppressed irritation came to a head in 1929, when troops had to be called in to restore order. Quiet was soon restored, but mutterings of discontent continued. A Commission of Inquiry was opened, and sat for a considerable time; but long before it ended the urgent need was realized for the setting up of some other local authority than that of the artificially created chiefs. These were removed—it was not their fault that they had ever been appointed—and, after most careful consideration, it was resolved that the traditional Village Councils should be put in their stead as Native Administrations. It was a brave decision to take, since the practical difficulties were weighty: the village areas would be so small as to lack adequate public funds, expenditure on essential salaries would be hard to meet, development schemes requiring public outlay might be indefinitely delayed, many of the Councils would be almost absurdly unwieldy in size, and the native courts would in many instances have more judges present than prisoners, officials, and onlookers put together! But the system was to be tried out. If the Northern Provinces startled the Empire by adopting Native Administration through local chiefs, the Eastern Provinces astonished everyone, including themselves, by granting power to Councils closely resembling public meetings.[1] But the confidence, it has turned out, was not misplaced, and now that there is a prospect of a measure of eventual federation of districts, the financial drawbacks of too exiguous local areas are likely to be reduced. And, after all, too exiguous districts are not confined to the Village Councils system, but also exist in certain of the Northern Provinces.

Thus in parts of Nigeria the chiefs are being trained in responsible local self-government, and in other parts the Village Councils. The only standing difficulty—and it is useless to ignore it—is the serious amount of bribery and corruption prevailing. A good deal of this may be discounted on the ground that some rake-off is expected in all African transactions, as it has always been the custom to give some return for services expected to be rendered. But there is still an unfortunate residue. It is impossible to give any estimate of its extent, but certainly there is a great deal that is not justified by custom and that is a gross trading on official position. On the other hand there is not much extortion, that is, forcing money or property unjustly from people. The whole problem is a ticklish one, and there is no panacea for it. The District Officer has simply to keep his eyes constantly open for the least sign of malpractice, and to deal with it if he can find evidence. The chief danger spot lies in the assessment and collection of taxes, where there is abundant scope for acquiring more than is just.

[1] For the whole question of local administration in Nigeria, the reader is referred to *Native Administration*, by Margery Perham (Oxford University Press).

It is indeed the D.O.'s most exacting duty, in which extraordinary refinements of cunning and ingenuity have to be met with ingenuity no less refined.

For the supervision of local administration and the working of the native courts the District Officer or his A.D.O. has to be frequently on tour, when he is accessible to complaints of all kinds, from the slightly unbalanced type, through the determined and timid (who come like Nicodemus by night with their faces veiled), to the determined and bold. Personal motives are apt to weigh heavily, and the Officer's judgment becomes of first importance. He can seldom believe anything he is told, but has to differentiate exactly between fine shades of lies (and with experience at length he can do so). Only thus can he succeed in administration at all. It is a most difficult task.

Chapter Nine

ON WAR SERVICE

NIGERIA seems so remote from Europe that one might well be excused for wondering whether the war had affected it at all. In fact, not only did the war affect Nigeria greatly, but to some extent Nigeria affected the course of the war.

A Colony, and for that matter a Protectorate too, becomes automatically at war when the home country does. Nor, when the possibility of war has been foreseen for some time, does it enter without preparation. The plan of defence of ports and key positions is laid down, so that on the declaration of war it is merely a matter of giving the word to go, and units move into place, barbed wire springs up, bayonets glisten, and machine-guns occupy their nests. The Colonial Attorney-General drafts Defence Regulations granting essential powers, and these are set up in type ready for printing off at a moment's notice. Instructions are issued to people in remote places, so that they will know the part they are to play, and telegrams to them are written out ready for dispatch when the time comes. Streams of telegrams in cipher flow between the Colonial Office in London and the Governor of the Colony, conveying behind-the-scenes information, estimates of probabilities and possibilities, and detailed instructions and guidance. New services come into being, like the censorship and shipping control. (Few people realize that there are only three British Colonies without direct access to the sea, viz., Northern Rhodesia, Nyasaland, and Uganda, and only four whose capital is not also a port, viz., the same three and Kenya. The life of the Colonies so depends on the sea that much of the preparation for war is necessarily concerned with ports and shipping.) The Cipher Section of the Secretariat had to deal with all the communications in and out, working by shifts twenty-four hours a day. At the start most of this work was done by men who were already working at high pressure all day, and some of them manning machine-guns every other night. But a team of volunteer European women was enlisted, and they eventually took over the whole of the ciphering.

As for military preparations, the appropriate employment of West African troops had to be borne in mind, namely, for campaigns in tropical countries, and since our most likely enemy in Africa was Italy, the Nigerian troops were trained for use, if necessary, against the Italians in East Africa. During times of peace Nigeria had six excellent battalions of infantry, a battery of small calibre artillery, and a detachment of signals. There were no ancillary troops. The units formed part of the R.W.A.F.F.[1] covering the four West African Colonies.

The Nigeria Regiment is normally a unit in the private army of the Colonial Office, and does not come under the War Office ; it is a Department of the Nigerian Government just as Medical and Education are. It is paid for by the Nigerian taxpayer, since it is concerned with internal security rather than external wars, or even the defence of Nigeria against external enemies. The wonder is that its 3,000 odd bayonets suffice to maintain order among over twenty million people, of whom part are as yet scarcely settled.

On the declaration of war the first thing the regiment had to do was to call its reservists back to the colours and to organize war-service recruiting, and the next was to train African recruits and new British officers and non-commissioned officers. But this expansion was only justified if we were to fight Italy. If Italy did not come into the war

[1] Royal West African Frontier Force

there was really no need for expansion, since there was then no theatre of war suitable for African troops; and in fact, at the beginning of course, Italy did not do so. So the Commandant was left in the air, not knowing what to do. Italy might come in at any moment, when the Nigerian troops would be wanted, but on the other hand Italy might stay out indefinitely, and then Nigerian preparations would only mean locking up equipment and officers badly needed elsewhere.

In the end the usual middle course was followed; a certain proportion of European civil staff was released for military service, and recruiting began for specialist corps. As a result there were soon a signals unit, a corps of mechanical transport, a survey unit, field companies of sappers, and a field ambulance. All these had African other ranks with British officers, of whom some came from Britain and Rhodesia, but most were found locally.

Meanwhile the defence of the vital port of Lagos rested on the rifles and machine-guns of the local volunteer Defence Force, an entirely European body, together with a Territorial company of Africans. Every third night in turn they manned their machine-guns and held their breath. Fortunately nothing happened, though the troops were full of vain dreams of immediate honour and glory.

Nigeria being surrounded on three sides by French Colonies and on the fourth by the sea, it was on the fourth alone that there was apparent prospect of danger. Though many were scornful at the time, there is little doubt that even a brief occupation by, say, the crew of an enemy cruiser would have caused serious dislocation in the country, and have had propaganda value to the Germans quite out of proportion to its importance. But however awkward this would have been for the time, there was no fear of permanent invasion from the sea, nor was Nigeria within enemy air range.

Threat to Nigeria

The first year of the war dragged on, and then came the crash with the fall of France. Henceforth Nigeria instead of being safely surrounded by friendly territory, found itself hemmed in by country doubtful in its immediate intentions, and only too likely to become hostile before long. Moreover, the Italians having at length come into the war, the Nigeria Brigade was needed to fight in East Africa. The defence of West Africa now became a matter for grave consideration. Recruiting was intensified, there were increasing releases from the Government service, and compulsory training in the Defence Force was introduced. White troops began arriving in Nigeria as fast as they could be spared from Britain. The Coast bristled with Colonels, and as some said, Lagos was crowded with Colonels, Half-Colonels, and Palm Kernels. Anti-aircraft defence became something more than academic as men were landed who had shot down planes off Hull two months before, and Air Raid Precautions were instituted in the more vital centres.

Sea losses and the diversion of shipping began to put a serious strain on food supply from overseas, and Food Control was started in earnest. Petrol control was tightened up. Then Transport Control made a determined but involved attempt to check unnecessary traffic on the roads. The new duties put an immense weight of extra work on the shoulders of the Provincial Headquarters staffs, already depleted and still with all their normal work to do. European women helped a great deal in manning these controls ; indeed without them the situation would have been impossible. At first their services were voluntary, but later, when the work was made compulsory, they received a small amount of pay.

Since paper was likely to become scarce a Committee

examined the possibilities of retrenchment, and checking over the 3,000 current Government forms they found that they could save 40 per cent. by rearrangement and using smaller sizes of type. But a good deal of this saving was cancelled out by the printed matter issued for the controls and other new activities.

A big drive took place to get both white people and educated Africans to " live on the country " instead of on imports. In peace-time many used in any case to take provisions with them ; but others bought from local firms imported tinned and bottled foods to eke out the meat supplied from the cold storage. Such travellers obtained a certain amount of green stuff locally, but most of their eating was out of an imported tin. The drive against this habit was successful, and a book published in Jos, called *Live on the Country*, led many people to try using ingredients they had previously scarcely heard of.

The Government itself took a hand and on the Plateau started butter-making, then cheese-making, and finally pig-keeping. Most of the butter, cheese, bacon, and ham went to the troops, as was right and proper, but the civilians were allotted a share. Thus we saved importing a large quantity of food from Britain. It is true that in some ways we were living better than the people there, but we were short of all the luxuries that used to make life in the Tropics comfortable. We also became short of things that were not short in Britain, for example, flour and salt ; and at one time supplies of kerosene fell very low. But the salt shortage was the most serious, since Africans consume salt in large quantities.

The troops had to be fed, and they required huge supplies of meat, grain, and eggs. Vegetables and fruit had to be provided for them in places where there had been little production before ; and one small station typically found itself due to supply a quarter of a ton of vegetables a day !

Air Reinforcement Route

When the French Chad Territory came into the war on the Allied side—and that was probably the turning point in our fortunes, since if Chad had remained with Vichy the British hold on Egypt would have been gravely imperilled—it became possible to use the old British Air Mail Route across Central Africa to the Middle East. It was not to fly letters that it was reopened, but to fly fighter planes, urgent spares, and essential officials. The Air Route runs from Accra to Lagos, then to Kano, with lesser airfields at Oshogbo, Minna, and Kaduna, and on to Maiduguri. From Maiduguri it goes to Fort Lamy in Chad Territory, El Geneina in the Sudan, and so to Khartoum; thence either east, south, or north. This was the key supply line. Later alternatives were developed as relief lines, but that remained the quickest (and least comfortable). At dinner in Maiduguri one could hear news from London, chat from Cairo, gossip from Chungking, and the latest from Pretoria and Washington.

The opening of this route meant that R.A.F. detachments had to be posted along it for maintenance, wireless, weather observation, and so on, and these troops required large camps and special food supplies. Millions of gallons of petrol had to be moved enormous distances by road. When the Americans came on to the route they made their own camps but used our airfields, where they were very easy to work with and always ready to co-operate.

Flying over Africa has always been hazardous, since it is not possible to make a forced landing with much chance of success, yet the number of R.A.F. planes lost in such landings was surprisingly small. One plane crashed about thirty miles north of Potiskum, between Kano and Maiduguri. When the R.A.F. rescue tender arrived they found a track had been cleared all the way from the main road : the pilot, slightly injured, had been lifted from his plane on to clean mats ; a dresser had been brought thirty miles to bandage him ; a small hut had been built over him where he lay ; and, to round off the picture, the village headman was fanning the flies off him !

The old airfields were enlarged at the beginning of the war, and again after 1940. New buildings for various purposes—guard rooms, quarters, hostels, canteens, offices, hospitals, stores, and garages—were run up in many parts of the country. All this building for the Navy, Army, and R.A.F. was done by the Public Works Department, who also still had their ordinary maintenance work to do, though admittedly the Army had sapper companies doing road work and helping with supervision.

The strain on the Department was immense, but they proved equal to it. Voluntary labour in bulk was employed on the airfields, buildings, and roads. One Province alone employed about 20,000 men at a time on war work, often at places that normally do not carry any great population, so that markets for food had to be set up and other services supplied, such as camps, police, and sanitary officials, drinking water, and transport.

The Railway had to stand up to strains undreamed of. Roads were reconstructed, and even new ones built, including the vast undertaking of a road from Maiduguri to Fort Lamy, through the deep swamps that at times are veritable lakes. For nearly a hundred miles this road runs on an embankment built to keep it above the water. There are a few small bridges over what pass for streams, but in fact the whole structure is a pier with neither stone nor steel, but solely piled-up mud.

War Production

Despite her forests and an export trade in fine woods, before the war Nigeria used to import some timber. She has now developed her own resources, and even exported. The Public Works Sawmill at Ijora near Lagos broke all records, and turned out furniture in vast quantities for the Forces, and so did every Public Works yard throughout the country : the Native Administration workshops did the same, and also provided an invaluable repair service on the very fringes of the desert both for the R.A.F. and for the Army. Ijora sawmill, too, made great numbers of sectional huts, which were sent along the Coast to other colonies for their garrisons.

In spite of new building programmes and the erection of temporary houses, the housing shortage was acute in most big centres, and two or three families had to live in one house. This may not sound a serious trial, and, of course, compared with what might have happened it is a trifle, yet it weighed on the people, since in tropical countries it is better for a man or a married couple to live alone, meeting other people when so inclined, but also being able to get away from them when necessary. Circumstances, too, led people to travel about much more than they had done in peace-time, and as they had to put up wherever they visited, this placed a heavy additional strain on housing, and increased the discomfort of a country that is uncomfortable even with all possible conveniences. In many stations it became necessary to have billeting schemes even for civilian travellers.

The Army meanwhile had been growing out of all recognition. The old comfortable R.W.A.F.F. had been engulfed in vast new formations. More and more white officers and N.C.Os. came out to train the African rank and file. On every side appeared new people, and some day much will be written on the achievements of these military forces. There is no need to write here of the magnificent feats of the Nigerian troops in East Africa, already celebrated in an excellent book on that campaign. These troops were the old regular battalions, the men one used before the war to see in their brilliant ceremonial parades, their colours flapping in the breeze, their faultless khaki and brave scarlet coats a joy to the eye, their band playing with a swing, a glory of scarlet and gold, their arms drill superb, and their timing perfect. These were the troops who raced up from the roasting plains of Mogadishu to the heights of Diredawa, and who fought grimly in the sickening gullies of the Omo River and the southern lakes of Abyssinia.

When in 1942 Malaya fell, Britain was faced with a shortage of many products hitherto obtained from there ; but Nigeria overhauled production and both increased it and extended its range. There was a drive to secure more oil seeds, ground nuts, palm oil, and rubber, besides kapok for life-saving gear and analphe silk for parachutes (analphe silk comes from a flat cocoon found on certain bush trees). String and rope were manufactured from local fibres instead of being imported. Bags for the transport of grain were made from palm fibre or from leather—the excellent leather of the north proved invaluable for many purposes. For the tin mines thirty thousand additional labourers were recruited, nearly doubling the normal labour force ; but this could only be achieved by quotas from each Province— fortunately tin-mining was the only form of labour for which compulsion had to be resorted to. The undertaking was a complicated one. Some of the men travelled by special train, some by lorry, and some walked, and when they were assembled their food supplies had to be organized and maintained, camps had to be built, and all services provided. Lord Swinton, as Resident Minister in West Africa, played a vital part in this great production drive by co-ordinating and inspiring the effort.

After two years of small rains, and consequent depletion of reserves of grain, food supplies for the Africans began to cause concern. A third bad year would have reduced the country to a state of famine. Fortunately the 1942 Rains, though meagre enough, proved sufficient. A central authority to buy corn was set up, and a threefold distribution was organized, namely, for the troops, the mining area, and the reserve for civilian needs. Storage for all the grain acquired presented its own problems. Various methods of storage had to be employed, according to regional custom and climatic conditions : in some parts granaries were built of matting and thatch raised above the ground on sticks, in others deep pits were dug, roofed with thatch, lined with chaff and matting, and protected by low walls with padlocked doors.

One afternoon Fort Lamy had an air raid. A German aeroplane from Murzuk flew the length of Lake Chad, lost its way for a while, and then, recovering its bearings, swung off to the Shari and Fort Lamy. Arriving at siesta-time, it dropped its bombs and got off as the first round was fired by the rather dazed crew of a Bofors gun. One of its bombs unfortunately hit a large dump of petrol brought five hundred miles by road from Jos, there were two or three minor casualties, and all was over.

The fat was now in the fire : a partial black-out was added to previous tribulations, and batteries of anti-aircraft guns were rushed up from the coast with enormous labour and credit to the gunners. The black-out was a nuisance ; it was never satisfactory. It caused a great deal of unpleasantness between the R.A.F. and the Americans on the one side, who both thought it unnecessary, and the Administration on the other, who had to see that it was carried out. It was difficult to see what good it did in the wide spaces of Africa.

The best commentary on the whole thing was the fact that the Free French at Fort Lamy, where all the trouble had started, did not have one themselves. " Nous n'avons pas ici un *black-out*," they would say a little wistfully, as though they were missing something.

In addition to all our other work and worries we had to report the progress of the war to the local Africans. This was done by talks in towns and villages, by printed matter for those who could read, and in the larger towns by information kiosks and reading rooms where pictures and maps were displayed. While the simple farmer took little interest in the war—for war is so much a matter of geography—the people in the towns followed it intently. It was curious to see in Maiduguri how the crowds at the Shehu's gate varied with our success. A victory would bring several thousands to the talk, a defeat—and we never minimized defeats— would reduce it to a few hundreds ; but there was always a substantial number present. None ever had any doubt of ultimate Allied victory ; indeed our trouble was the wide- spread complacency, and we had a hard task to persuade the crowds that victory could only be gained by blood, sweat, and toil. The talks were backed up by posters and pictures, but the ordinary African cannot readily understand still pictures (moving pictures with a familiar background are easier for him). Moreover, unusual angles in still pictures are a special stumbling block. An intelligent and educated African when shown an excellent air photo of the flight deck of the *Illustrious*—the carrier lying across centre, and sea appearing above and below—at once asked, " What sank the carrier ? " When assured that it was not sunk, but floating normally, he protested, " But how can it be afloat with sea above it and sea below it ? " Still, by one means and another, the news and the message never failed in the end to get across.

War Finance

As in other countries the Nigerian tax-payer has helped a good deal by the simple though painful process of paying taxes quickly and on first demand. In many areas notably shy in the past in the matter of tax payment money came through quite promptly. Obviously there was more money about, but that by itself is not sufficient explanation of such a thorough-going change.

Collections for charities were started soon after the war began and have been going on ever since. By the end of 1944 the total collected was £125,000, of which the Nigerian Troops Comforts Fund received a good share. One of the more original charitable efforts was the Windcheater Fund organized by two ladies in Lagos who collected money and with it bought sheepskins, which were turned into much appreciated jerkins for sailors on the small ships of the Navy.

The *Nigeria Daily Times*, published in Lagos by an African company, started a " Win the War Fund " for the purchase of war weapons. This was generously subscribed to from all over the country. The sums received may not seem very large having regard to the population of the country, but the African is not used to the idea of giving to charities or subscribing money, charity very definitely beginning and ending with the large home unit, and there had to be no suspicion of pressure in appealing for the money. The danger of pressure is perhaps difficult to appreciate by those outside Africa, but the fact is that the ordinary African tends to take a suggestion by a European not as an open matter but as an order. The Germans accused us of getting money for these collections by forced levy, but far from that there was not the remotest trace of abuse of influence.

I remember how in Bornu the Shehu of his own initiative

expressed his wish to give a Spitfire to the King, not to the R.A.F., but to the King—a purely personal affair—and said that the people would like to contribute. I agreed provided that no pressure of any kind was used and that the maximum accepted from any person should be 2d. That sounds very little, but as at that time a man could live in Bornu Province quite well on 4d. a day, it was half a day's keep. The money came in very quickly and the Spitfire was bought. When next I went on tour I checked up on this collection, in case there had been any abuse, but found no trace of it. In places people had not been quite certain what the money was intended for, but they said it was something to help the King in the war and they were glad to give it, and if he wanted any more he had only to ask. And indeed in the long run they and the other Provinces had paid for a complete fighter squadron, bombers, tanks, canteens, and many other war supplies.

When the East African campaign ended the Nigerian troops returned home. After further intensive training the 81st Division, which is two-thirds Nigerian, went to India, to the Kaladan Valley, where they did well, and won respect as fighters even from the Gurkhas, not to mention the Japanese. A Nigerian Brigade comprised in the Chindit force excelled itself. Nigerian Pioneers went to North Africa, and African dressers to Italy. Later a second Division, the 82nd, also went to India, where they acquitted themselves as well as the 81st had done. Thus did people who had never heard of Nigeria become neighbours of Nigerians, and Nigerians saw fresh places and new things.

10a

Chapter Ten

WHAT THEN?

So much for the past, for what has been done in Nigeria, for what it was and what it is. But what is it going to be?

Nigeria has done a great deal in the face of considerable odds, both financial and physical; financial because she has had to stand on her own feet without help from the Home Treasury, and physical, too, because the European out there often loses drive under Nigerian conditions. It is unhappily true that the European, unless a rare exception, after some years becomes enervated and dispirited, with an inevitable tendency to continue in the path he knows best and not to strike out afresh. This physical drawback of the climate cannot easily be counterbalanced, but the financial strains have been eased by the revolutionary Colonial Development and Welfare Act of 1944 which made comparatively large sums available for special expenditure. Big schemes at length become possible—and big schemes do not imply extravagant schemes. In a large country even simple plans may have to be carried out on such a scale that they automatically become large-scale ones. For example, if it were decided to spend the small sum of £100 per village on, say, sanitation, the total that would have to be reckoned on for the whole country would be at least £2,000,000.

Plans are now being made for the fuller development of Nigeria as soon as material and staff become available. But even planning in so large a Colony is not easy. Other Colonies have been able to produce completed plans quite early in the day. They have been able to do so either because problems were simpler or just because they are smaller and more workable in size. So much has to be considered in Nigeria, so many factors come into play, so many diversities of culture and climate exist, that it is not possible to produce plans quickly ; and in any event forced speed would only cause mistakes and waste.

Physically there will be definite future progress for all Nigerians, particularly through the lessons learnt in dealing with the welfare and health of the troops of all nations stationed in tropical countries during the war, and this will apply especially to those responsible for the development and administration of the country, both African and European. Moreover, the improvements in communications and amenities that can reasonably be expected should increase the keenness and capacity of the whites living in Nigeria. A further factor will exert its influence, namely, that the Europeans will suffer less from *fear* of ill health, which has hitherto been a strong contributory factor to ill health proper, for they too often went out with a feeling that they were going to the white man's graveyard if not to the grave itself. In time Nigeria will be a better and healthier country to live in, though never a paradise.

The moderate African groups express to-day a reasonable and genuine desire for more definite control by Africans over national expenditure and a greater share of the higher Government posts, at present held for the most part by Europeans. They do not ask for sudden and total independence, but for self-government within the Empire. There is a tendency to demand a time limit for the change-over, but this is due to an understandable weariness of past delays and indecision. The greatest obstacle to the granting of even a measure of self-government is the complexity of the problem, when a square deal for all is intended, for the various parts of the country are at quite different stages of development and political consciousness. Education will be able to do much to remedy the disparities, as and when suitable schemes have been thought out and organized ; but academic or craft teaching alone will be powerless without an integration of all factors—physical, mental, social, and moral—and no satisfactory programme has yet been devised. Meanwhile stability and harmony are greater than the forces of unrest, there is no dislike of the European as such, and there is a widespread and very strong personal loyalty to the Crown. News of the Royal Family is always eagerly received, and royal visits are a great binding influence. The words of cabinet ministers are attentively studied, and constructions are put upon them that would often surprise their authors. Governors and other officials with high responsibility are greatly respected. There is a touching pride among the mass of Africans in belonging to the Empire.

But in spite of all this, and the advances in means of transport and communication, the amount of knowledge spread throughout the country is disappointingly small, whether it is knowledge of Nigeria itself and the peoples who live there, or about Great Britain, or about the Dominions, or about other parts of the Empire, even those in West Africa itself. Until the prevailing ignorance is changed to knowledge, little can be done to get the populace to think and plan. The bulk of the people are still very parochial and conservative.

Yet it is probable that only on this solid basis of " village sanity," the product of a steady sense of human nature, that a stable future for Nigeria can be founded. Every dictate of self-interest and a large measure of popular sentiment recommend continued membership of the Empire. Nigeria cannot make headway without British skill, guidance, money, and protection ; neither, on the other hand, can the government of Nigeria be effective without the great army of African clerks, craftsmen, and technicians now employed, and the greater army still that in due course the development plans will inevitably call into existence. As time goes on, more and more responsible posts will naturally be filled by Africans, and a solid body of public opinion will arise.

With courageous and far-sighted leadership on the part of both Africans and Europeans, and the close and understanding support of the British people and Government, much can and will be done. Light can be brought to the dark places of the land, water can be made to spring up in the thirsty plains, health and strength can be given to the millions no longer hopelessly suffering, and prosperity and happiness can one day prevail among these patient people; but only if all work together for the good of all.

Britain has given the world a living example of what "Empire" should mean—flexibility with interdependence. She can now show how out of diversity may come strength, out of apparent confusion harmony, and out of almost insuperable difficulties triumphs greater than those of war. But nothing can be achieved without co-operation and mutual understanding. A chord pleases more than a single note: each note takes its appointed place, there is no pre-eminence or self-seeking, each contributes its proper share to the final harmony.

BOOKS FOR FURTHER READING

Barth, Dr., *Travels in Central Africa* (Longmans)

Basden, G. T., *Among the Ibos of Nigeria* (Seeley Service)

Bovill, E. W., *Caravans of Old Sahara* (Oxford University Press)

Burns, A. C., *History of Nigeria* (Allen and Unwin)

Haig, E. F. G., *Nigerian Sketches* (Allen and Unwin)

Hailey, Lord, *African Survey* (Oxford University Press)

Hall, T. H. D., *Barrack and Bush in Northern Nigeria* (Allen and Unwin)

Hastings, A. C. G., *Voyage of the " Dayspring "* (Lane)

Hives, Frank, *Juju and Justice in Nigeria* (Lane)

Hogben, S. J., *Muhammadan Emirates of Nigeria* (Oxford University Press)

Kingsley, Mary, *Travels in West Africa* (Macmillan)

Langa-Langa, *Up against it in Nigeria* (Allen and Unwin)

Lugard, Lady, *A Tropical Dependency* (Nisbet)

Lugard, Lord, *Dual Mandate in Tropical Africa* (Blackwood)

Meek, C. K., *Northern Tribes of Nigeria* (Oxford University Press) ; *A Sudanese Kingdom* (Kegan Paul) ; *Tribal Studies in N. Nigeria* (Kegan Paul)

Mockler-Ferryman, *British Nigeria* (Cassell)

Niven, C. R., *A Short History of Nigeria* (Longmans)

Oakley, R. R., *Treks and Palavers* (Seeley Service)

Park, Mungo, *Travels in Africa* (Dent, Oxford University Press)

Perham, M., *Native Administration in Nigeria* (Oxford University Press)

Simpson, Helen, *A Woman among Wild Men* (Nelson)

Talbot, P. A., *Peoples of S. Nigeria* (Oxford University Press) ; *Tribes of the Niger Delta* (Sheldon Press)

MAPS AND CHARTS

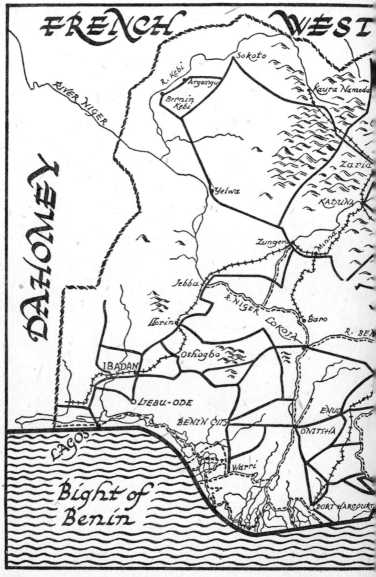

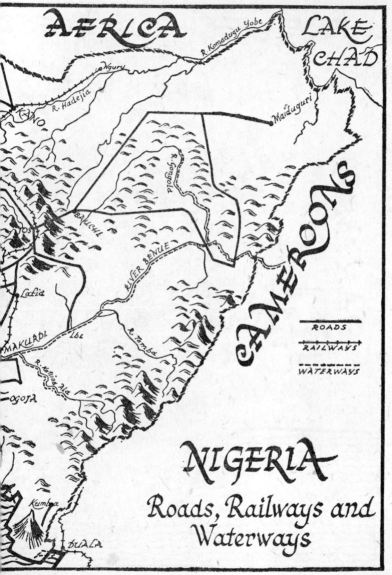

AFRICA

R. Komadugu Yobe

LAKE CHAD

Nguru

R. Hadejia

KANO

Maiduguri

R. Gongola

BAUCHI

JOS

RIVER BENUE

CAMEROONS

Lafia

MAKURDI   Ibi

R. Tamba

R. Katsina Ala

OGOJA

ROADS
RAILWAYS
WATERWAYS

Kumba

DUALA

NIGERIA
Roads, Railways and
Waterways

FRENCH WEST

RIVER NIGER

DAHOMEY

Lokoja

E

T

S

Lagos

Calabar

Bight of Benin

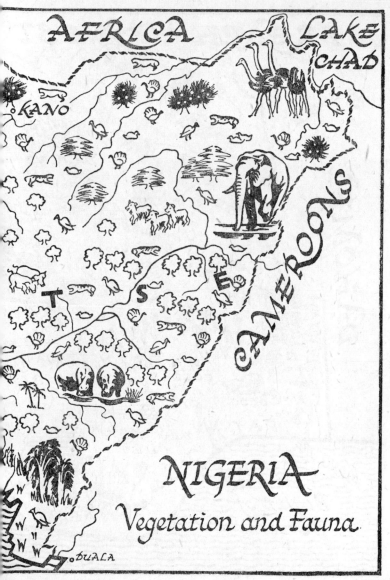

AFRICA LAKE CHAD

KANO

CAMEROONS

NIGERIA

Vegetation and Fauna

DUALA

FRENCH WEST

DAHOMEY

RIVER NIGER

R. Kebi

RICE

GROUND NUTS

Cotton

Guinea Corn

GOLD

Shea Nuts

Rice

Ginger

Ropes

R. NIGER

Guinea Corn

R. BENUE

Cotton

TIN

Plantains

LOKOJA

Yams

COAL

Yams

Rice

GOLD

PALMS

KERNELS

Cocoa

Cassava

Yams

Cassava

Yams

PALM OIL &

FURNITURE

Coal

Plantains

Bight of Benin

KERNELS

154

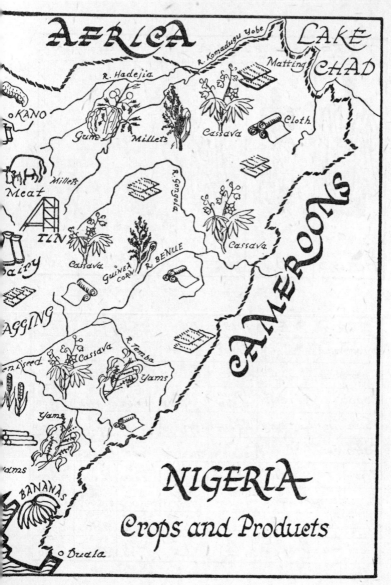

AFRICA

LAKE CHAD

R. Komadugu Yobe

Matting

R. Hadejia

o KANO

Gum

Millets

Cassava

Cloth

Millets

Meat

R. Gongola

TIN

Cassava

Cassava

DAIRY

GUINEA CORN

R. BENUE

BAGGING

Cassava

R. Tenba

Yams

Linseed

Yams

CAMEROONS

Yams

BANANAS

o Duala

NIGERIA

Crops and Products

155

TRIBES — FIGURES ALL IN THOUSANDS

3,604	3,172	3,766	930	750
Hausa	Ibo	Yoruba	Kanuri	Ibibio

TRADE	1918	1924	1930	1936	1943
Imports Value (IN THOUSANDS)	£7,422	£10,948	£12,617	£6,500	£12,418
Exports Value	£9,522	£14,460	£15,029	£9,000	£15,151
Cocoa TONS	10,279	37,200	52,300	80,500	87,000
Palm kernels TONS	205,167	252,850	260,000	386,000	331,000
Palm oil	86,425	127,000	135,000	135,000	162,000
Tin TONS	8,300	8,850	12,000	12,000	17,500
Groundnuts TONS	57,550	78,000	146,000	218,000	142,000
Cattle hides	—	—	2,390	2,500	2,580
Goats and sheep skins	—	—	2,470	4,300	3,680

INDEX

157

INDEX

158

INDEX

PRINTED IN GREAT BRITAIN AT THE PRESS OF THE PUBLISHERS